YOU DON'T SAY!

2

Barry Phelps is one of a vanishing breed, the polymath. He
has travelled, studied, read and written widely, and everything interests him – except team sports. His earlier books
have covered family finance, genealogy, literary criticism,
political history and biography, most recently the definitive
P. G. Wodehouse: Man and Myth. He has been a soldier,
stockbroker, *Daily Mail* journalist, banker, and magazine
editor, public relations executive and unemployed litigant.
In the course of his career he was briefly a millionaire, but
doesn't expect to regain that status by writing books for
intelligent people like the readers of *You Don't Say!*. He is a
bibliomaniac and his library is eclectic, in the worst sense of
the word. His favourite pastime is keeping a straight face
while teasing people with no sense of humour. At present he
is a councillor of the Royal Borough of Kensington &
Chelsea, representing the Earl's Court ward where he lives,
and is writing a biography of Stanley Baldwin which, he
promises, 'will offend everyone'.

You Don't Say!

THE DICTIONARY OF
MISQUOTATIONS

BARRY PHELPS

MACMILLAN

First published 1995 by Macmillan Reference Books

a division of Macmillan Publishers Ltd
25 Eccleston Place London SW1W 9NF
and Basingstoke

Associated companies throughout the world

ISBN 0 333 63825 5

1 3 5 7 9 8 6 4 2

A CIP catalogue record for this book is available from
the British Library

Typeset by CentraCet Limited, Cambridge
Printed and bound by
Cox & Wyman Ltd, Reading, Berkshire

For my children
Rupert and Cecily or Cecily and Rupert
They can fight it out between them

CONTENTS

Acknowledgements

ix

Introduction

xi

Misquotations A–Z

1

Frequently Cited and Consulted Sources

175

Index of Key Words and Phrases

179

Source Notes

193

ACKNOWLEDGEMENTS

JAMES DUFFICY was of enormous help to me in compiling this book, carrying out much research and writing a number of the entries. Without him *You Don't Say!* would not have been completed. However he takes no responsibility for my asides, emendations and opinions. Nor do the following friends and strangers whose helpful suggestions and advice I gratefully acknowledge.

Giles Bartleet of Martini-Rossi; Paul F. Boller Jr. and John George for permission to cite from *They Never Said It*; the British Library staff at Bloomsbury and Colindale; Bill Bryson, whose fascinating book, *Made In America*, yielded several useful misquotations; Lucinda Buxton of the Savoy Hotel press office; David Cash of *Private Eye*; Noel Clarke, proto-European; David Cooper, my solicitor; David Damant; Ann Dewe, ace literary agent, for much constructive criticism of my early draft and great professionalism; John Ebblewhite; Sally Edgecombe, the Johnson authority of Clarke-Hall booksellers; Nicholas Faith; Christopher Fildes; John Fletcher, publisher and polymath; Chris Glyn of the Foreign & Commonwealth Office news department; the ever-helpful, always delightful, Deborah Gray; Benny Green, the authority on musical theatre; Jonathon Green, the lexicographer, who was generous with his time, advice and friendship; Judith

Hannam, my invaluable editor at Macmillan; Val Hennessy of the *Daily Mail*.

Paul Hosefros, my cousin and senior photographer of the *New York Times*, Washington Bureau, was invaluable. Not only did he put me up in Washington while I worked in the Library of Congress but he later made good errors of omission and checked numerous points for me.

Hugh Johnson, all the world's wine adviser; Leslie Johnston, classicist and antiquarian book dealer; Alan Kennard especially; Rabbi James Kennard; Bernard Levin; Library of Congress staff, Washington DC; the London Library staff; Charles McCorquodale; Christopher Makey, barrister-at-law; Norman Murphy, author of *In Search Of Blandings*; New York City Library staff; Revd Canon David Painter; my son Rupert; Stella Rennocks; my daughter Cecily Roberts; Gerald W. Scott, who is too wise to be called cynical; Godfrey Smith of the *Sunday Times*; Colin Smythe, the Yeats authority and bibliographer; Sir William van Straubenzee MBE; Rt. Hon. Lord Tebbit CH; Barnaby Williams, writer of epic thrillers.

B.P.

INTRODUCTION

The urge to quote is nicely matched by the tendency to misquote.

That urge is born in us. Quotations are often coded recognition symbols between people of similar backgrounds – whether classics scholars or football hooligans. They may be a form of shorthand, compressing a whole argument into a few words. They bring notable reinforcements to help in debate. It may be no more than showing off – and a harmless piece of one-upmanship.

The tendency to misquote is equally innate. Journalists, especially sub-editors writing headlines, seek brevity: sometimes this is an improvement on the original, often it robs it of any nuance, balance and subtlety it may have had. Some quotations get bowdlerized or corrupted as they pass by word of mouth. Others get vulgarized. Perennial quotations change from one era to the next. Gresham's Law applies to quotations but not consistently: the bad do drive out the good, but occasionally the better drives out the worse.

Prominent wits – Rochester, Sheridan, Wilde, Shaw, Woollcott, Parker et al. – are apt to have any current witticism ascribed to them in order to give the orphan quotation parentage in a censorious world.

Politicians and churchmen have always been the worst

offenders (greatest adepts?) at twisting or counterfeiting their opponents remarks. They are similarly adept at taking remarks out of context and reading into them meanings which are not there. (They are, of course, mere tyros at the game compared with publishers' publicists culling laudatory phrases from condemnatory reviews.)

Lastly there are dying words. These can often be a powerful legacy, but most people don't leave any – so market forces meet the need. Not only are dying words invented but they are invented to please the buyers; the bereaved and unbereaved heirs.

An apt quotation at the right moment enhances conversation. The correct quotation of something usually misquoted scores bonus points. This book enables you to quote accurately and with confidence all the common, and many of the less common, misquotations. If something's worth quoting, it's worth quoting accurately.

And if something's worth misquoting it should be done with malice aforethought.

Misquotations

A-Z

A

Lord Acton (Sir John Acton Bt., 1st Baron Acton of Aldenham, 1834–1902), diplomat and historian.

In a letter to Mandell Creighton, later Bishop of London, Acton wrote: 'Power tends to corrupt and absolute power corrupts absolutely.'[1] That precisely weighted aphorism has been trimmed by less balanced minds to '*All power corrupts, absolute power corrupts absolutely*' – which manages to be untrue and trite at the same time. Creighton was the bishop who noted: 'No people do so much harm as those who go about doing good.'[2] William Pitt, 1st Eart of Chatham (q.v.), expressed the sentiment less well in the House of Lords on 9 January 1770. 'Unlimited power is apt to corrupt the minds of those who possess it.'

Gertrude Himmelfarb observed: 'Liberty too can corrupt, and absolute liberty can corrupt absolutely', which is true, but loses the elegance of Lord Acton's original.[3] Douglas Cater noted that 'If power corrupts, being out of power corrupts absolutely.'[4]

John Adams, *see* James Otis

Joseph Addison (1672–1719), man of letters, is often accused of writing '*He who hesitates is lost.*' Today, with the Equal Opportunities Commission ever vigilant, no man (*sic*) would dare quote Addison correctly, 'The woman that deliberates is lost.'[5]

Aesop (*c.* 620–560 BC), a Phrygian freedman, did not write

Aesop's Fables. The tales are traditional and the earliest extant written versions are by Babrius (first or second century AD) who put them into Greek verse and from which Phaedrus translated them into Latin. Aesop certainly told tales with a moral but Richard Bentley in his *Dissertation on the Fables of Aesop* assigns to them an oriental origin.[6] And while on the subject of eponymous works, *The Vision of Piers Plowman* is not one of them either – being written by William or Robert Langland around 1366. Nor is Sir John Manderville (1300–72) the author of *The Marvellous Adventures of Sir John Manderville* which are baldly taken from many sources but mainly cribbed from Friar Odoric (*floreat* 1330).[7] *See also* Joe Miller *and* Baron Munchhausen.

Spiro T. Agnew (1918–), vice-president to Richard Nixon, whose sense of ethics he shared.

The man who derided the press as an '. . . effete corps of impudent snobs who characterize themselves as intellectuals', and the 'nattering nabobs of negativism' (a line written for him by William Safire)[8] was never likely to receive positive treatment from the media. They portrayed him as a buffoon quoting such remarks as *'If you've seen one city slum, you've seen them all.'* In context Agnew said: 'I didn't say I wouldn't go into ghetto areas. I've been in many of them and to some extent I would have to say this: if you've seen one city slum you've seen them all.'[9] In America the vocation of corrupt politician is highly competitive with no room for fools and buffoons. Agnew was neither, but an intelligent crook who got caught.

Katherine Whitehorn, the *Observer* columnist, applied the reverse of such thinking to films. 'I wouldn't say that when you've seen one Western you've seen the lot; but when you've seen the lot you get the feeling you've seen one.'[10]

Pope Alexander VI, *see* Graham Greene

Muhammad Ali (born Cassius Marcellus Clay Jr., 1942–). The former world heavyweight boxing champion did not coin his famous maxim *'Float like a butterfly, sting like a bee'*, with its less familiar ending: *'Your hands can't hit what your eyes can't see.'*[11] The author was Ali's friend and assistant trainer, Drew 'Bundini' Brown, one of the few poets to be discharged from the American navy for attacking an officer with a meat cleaver. The television front man, Eammon Andrews, said: 'He stings like a bee but lives like a WASP'*[12] but Mr Andrews was not known for his wit and the credit belongs to his anonymous scriptwriter. In 1967 the admirable Ali courageously refused, on religious grounds, to be drafted to fight in Vietnam – and was stripped of his world heavyweight title. Twenty-five years later Americans voted a draft-dodger into the White House – *autre temps, autre mœurs*, as they say in Little Rock, Arkansas.

Woody Allen (Alan Stewart Konigsberg), *see* Humphrey Bogart

General Amru, *see* the Caliph Omar

Eammon Andrews, *see* Muhammad Ali

Anon. This prolific author has taken the credit for many verbal gems rightly the property of others. One of these is the advice, based on the politically correct view that all men are beasts and 'only interested in one thing', to *'Shut your eyes and think of England.'* Queen Victoria was, it is said, given

---

* White Anglo-Saxon Protestant.

3

similar advice on her wedding day. But it was Lady Hillingdon, in 1912, whose diary is the earliest instance I can find of the sentiment expressed in such patriotic terms: 'I am happy now that Charles calls in my bedchamber less frequently than of old. As it is, I endure but two calls a week, and when I hear his steps outside my door I lie down on my bed, close my eyes, open my legs and think of England.'[13] It can't have been much fun for Charles either.

Most people know of the Victorian rule that books by male and female authors should not abut each other on the same shelf. Few, if any, know the correct injunction, author and date. It is not Victorian, and is: 'The perfect hostess will see to it that the works of male and female authors be properly separated on the bookshelves. Their proximity, unless they happen to be married, should not be tolerated.' The author was Lady Gough, writing in her tome, *Etiquette*, in 1836 – before Victoria ascended the throne.

Anon. claims credit for 'The Army's Beatitude'. 'Blessed is he who expects nothing for he shall not be disappointed'. Alexander Pope (q.v.) wrote in 1725: 'I have a ninth Beatitude . . . Blessed is he who expects nothing for he shall never be disappointed'.[14] The same meal tastes far better when you expected poor fare rather than a fine repast.

Sometimes other authors take the credit for Anon.'s remarks: for one example, *see* Benjamin Disraeli on the Church of England. *See also* Edward H. Hoch *and* Andrew Jackson.

The Apostles, *see* Athanasius

Thomas Gold Appleton, *see* John Paul Jones

Mary and Jeffrey Archer, *see* Mr Justice Caulfield

Richard Armour, *see* Ogden Nash

Neil Armstrong (1930–), American astronaut. As Armstrong became the first man in human history to set foot on the moon, he made his famous remark: *'That's one small step for man, one giant leap for mankind'*, an obvious oddity since 'man' and 'mankind' are exact synonyms in that context.

This could be the most corrected quote of all time, but it still appears incorrectly as above instead of: 'That's one small step for a man, one giant leap for mankind.' The 'a' was lost to atmospherics during the 237,000-mile trip from the moon to Earth.[15]

But those were not the first words said on the moon, just the first quote! Buzz Aldrin, pilot of the Apollo module, spoke those first words on touchdown: 'Contact light.'[16]

Sir Robert Armstrong (from 1988 Lord Armstrong of Ilminster, 1927–), Secretary to the Cabinet 1979–87.

Sir Robert epitomized the Eton and Oxford career civil servant, even maintaining his urbanity in the alien milieu of an Australian court. On 18 November 1986 he was testifying on behalf of the British government, then attempting to suppress Peter Wright's unremarkable book *Spycatcher*. During cross-examination it was shown that a letter of Sir Robert's appeared to contain lies. He responded: 'It contains a misleading impression, not a lie. As one person said, it is perhaps being economical with the truth.' This was reported as '*I was being economical with the truth*', and greeted by the press as a neat new epigram*, but Sir Robert was better read. Edmund Burke (q.v.) wrote: 'Falsehood and delusion

---

* Or new neologism! It was that great editor of the *Daily Express*, Arthur Christiansen, who allegedly told his staff: '*What I want in this paper is new clichés.*' Christiansen is also credited with: '*We must avoid clichés like the plague.*'

are allowed in no case whatsoever. But, as in the exercise of all the virtues, there is an economy of truth.'[17]

Similar sentiments go back as far as Plato. 'The rulers of states are the only ones who should have the privilege of lying, either at home or abroad; they may be allowed the lie for the good of the state.'[18] Mark Twain (q.v.) said: 'Truth is the most valuable thing we have. Let us economize it.'[19] Sir Robert was making an elegant point on the use of language and also displaying his knowledge of moral theology, in which Cardinal Newman defined economy as 'cautious dispensation of the truth, after the manner of a discreet and vigilant steward'.[20] Such elitist points were not appreciated within the more robust atmosphere of the Australian court.

The problem recurs. On 8 March 1994 a British Cabinet minister, William Waldegrave, was asked by the Treasury & Civil Service Committee of MPs if it was ever acceptable for ministers to lie to Parliament. A nanosecond's reflection would have warned him that 'yes' and 'no' were equally disastrous answers. He replied, in effect, 'yes'. The correct response was to waffle, but it seems the minister lacked the guile required to do so. Cynics will feel it appropriate that Mr Waldegrave was the minister implementing the Conservative pledge of more open government.

President Carter kept his promise to the American people that he would never lie to them. President Nixon lied whenever he thought it useful. Nixon's first term is deemed great: Carter's only term is deemed ineffectual. Is there a moral there? I hope not.

Jean-Marie Arouet, *see* Voltaire

William, 3rd Viscount Astor, *see* Sir Robert Walpole

St Athanasius, Bishop of Alexandria (c. 296–373), did not write the Athanasian Creed which bears his name. It is probably the work of Caesarius (or Hilary), Bishop of Arles 503–43.[21]

Nor was the Apostles' Creed written by the Apostles – in spite of the charming legend that each of the twelve Apostles contributed one of its twelve verses. (As the four Gospels do not even agree on the names of the twelve Apostles, that begs further questions.) The Apostles' Creed is no older than the fifth century and took (roughly) its present form in the eighth century.[22]

If it is any comfort, the Nicene Creed did stem from the Conference of Nicaea in Bithynia, Asia Minor, in AD 325.

Rt. Hon. Clement R. Attlee (1st Earl Attlee, 1883–1967), *see* Winston L. S. Churchill

Alfred Austin (1835–1913), Poet Laureate, 1896–1913. Against stiff competition Austin remains one of the less inspiring of Britain's Poets Laureate with such couplets as . . .

> Low, where huge London, huger day by day,
> O'er six fair counties spreads its hideous sway[23]

. . . but he is innocent of the lines imperishably attributed to him and said to have been written during the illness of the Prince of Wales, later King Edward VII. *'Across the wires the electric message came/He is no better, he is much the same.'*[24] Another, unknown, pen wrote that – which at least rhymes and scans as, more or less, does John Bidlake's 'The sluggard carrot sleeps his day in bed/The crippled pea alone that cannot stand.'[25] However William Topaz McGonagall

(1825–1902) usually takes the title of Britain's worst published poet. His work still arouses strong emotions in the breasts of his fellow versifiers.

> Beautiful Railway Bridge of the Silv'ry Tay
> Alas, I am very sorry to say
> That ninety lives have been taken away
> On the last Sabbath day of 1879,
> Which will be remember'd for a very long time.[26]

Compare that with the following work of Julia Moore, the Sweet Singer of Michigan:

> Have you heard of the dreadful fate
> Of Mr P. P. Bliss and wife?
> Of their death I will relate,
> And also others lost their life
> In the Ashbula Bridge disaster,
> Where so many people died.[27]

Ms Moore presumably takes the American title. Her theme was always death, doom, disaster, destruction and despair: one critic noted that in a slim volume of verse, she had twenty-one people killed and nine wounded.

The life of one poet, George Wither (q.v.), was saved by the poverty of his muse. *See also* Ern Malley.

B

Francis Bacon (1561–1626), Baron Verulam and Viscount St Albans, peculant and lawyer, philosopher.

In his *Essays* Bacon wrote: 'The people assembled. Mahomet called the hill to come to him again and again; and when the hill stood still he was never a whit abashed but said "If the hill will not come to Mahomet, Mahomet will go to the hill".'[28] However the alliterative corruption '*If the mountain will not come to Mahomet, Mahomet will go to the mountain*', is more pleasing. This has a close affinity with King Canute (*c.* 994–1035): 'Being on the seashore [at Bosham] near Southampton, he sat down close to the rising tide and bade it go no further. When it advanced and wetted him, he said to his courtiers that they called him king, but that he "could not stay by his commandment so much as this small patch of water". This he did to reprove their flattery.'[29] As this story is also set at the Thames by Westminster and at the Wash, and can only be traced back to Henry, Archdeacon of Huntingdon (1084–1155) it, too, is probably apocryphal.

Baconians are vociferous in claiming that he wrote the works of Shakespeare.

'"What needs my Shakespeare for his honour'd bones? The labour of an Age in piled stones? Or that his hallowed Reliques should be hid, under a star-y pointing Pyramid ... As in the Plays and Sonnets we substitute the name equivalents of the total figure totals"' ... The Aunt inflated her lungs.

9

'These figure totals are always taken out in the Plain Cipher, A equalling one to Z equals twenty-four. A capital letter with the figures indicates an occasional variation in the name-count. For instance, A equals twenty-seven, B twenty-eight, until K equals ten is reached, when I, instead of ten becomes one and R or Reverse and so on, until A equals twenty-four is reached. The short or single digit is not used here. Reading the Epitaph in the light of the Cipher it becomes "What need of Verulam for Shakespeare? Francis Bacon England's King be hid under W. Shakespeare? William Shakespeare. Fame, what needest Francis Tudor, King of England? Francis, Francis W. Shakespeare. For Francis they William Shakespeare hath England's King took W. Shakespeare. Then thou our W. Shakespeare Francis Tudor bereaving Francis Bacon Francis Tudor such a tomb William Shakespeare".'

The speech was unusually simple and lucid for a Baconian.[30]

See also the Bible, Ben Jonson, John Milton *and* Alfred, Lord Tennyson

Stanley Baldwin (1st Earl Baldwin of Bewdley, 1867–1947), statesman; three times Prime Minister of Britain between 1923 and 1937.

Describing the new intake of MPs after the general election of 1918: *'They are a lot of hard-faced men who look as if they have done well out of the War.'*[31] This seemed apposite from Baldwin, recognized as a kind and philanthropic man who had been a wealthy ironmaster. John Maynard Keynes quoted it as said by 'a front-bench minister' who was taken to be Baldwin. Keynes seems to have paraphrased an observation of Baldwin's. 'They look much as usual; not so young as I had expected. The prevailing type is a rather successful-looking business kind which is not very attractive.'[32] This is a sentiment common to the more senior parliamentarians. The Duke of Wellington, upon seeing the MPs elected after the Great Reform Act of 1832, said: 'I never saw so many shocking bad hats in my life.'[33]

The press lords, Baron Beaverbrook and Viscount Rothermere, resented Baldwin's failure to accord them the access to 10 Downing Street they had enjoyed when David Lloyd George was premier. Baldwin finally routed both of them in a speech at the Queens Hall in London on 17 March 1931, in which he said: *What the proprietorship of these papers is aiming at is power, and power without responsibility – the prerogative of the harlot throughout the ages.*[34]* But the precept was given to Baldwin by his first cousin, Rudyard Kipling, who was godfather to Beaverbrook's son, Max. 'Naïvely bemused by the true nature of Lord Beaverbrook's ambitions, Kipling had asked directly what they were. "Power without responsibility," Beaverbrook had incautiously replied, and Kipling's devastating answer: "I see, the prerogative of the harlot throughout the ages" had been the death-knell of a long friendship.'[37] *See also* Lord Birkenhead, A. Bonar Law *and* Harold Macmillan.

Barabas, a publisher, *see* Lord Byron

Maurice Baring, *see* Hilaire Belloc

---

* Legend has it that a voice from the back of the hall, or perhaps the press table, shouted: 'There goes the harlot vote',[35] but legend is equally emphatic that the 9th Duke of Devonshire turned to his son-in-law, Harold Macmillan, and said: 'Good God. That's done it. He's lost us the tarts' vote.'[36]

George Barnes MP (1859–1940), a member of the War Cabinet in 1917, didn't actually say *'Hang the Kaiser'*,[38] in the old tradition of 'We'll give him a fair trial, then hang him.' What he said at a Labour Party meeting on 30 November 1918 was a tad less crude: 'I am in favour of hanging the Kaiser.' He omits this, his only notable phrase, from his memoirs, *From Workshop to War Cabinet*.

Phineas Taylor Barnum (1810–91), American showman. P. T. Barnum started his career in New York as a museum curator, with displays less educational than exhibitionist. Responsible for introducing the first freak shows and the famous General Tom Thumb, Barnum never understimated his audience; he knew exactly how low their tastes ran. It is no surprise then that *'You can fool all of the people some of the time and some of the people all the time, but you cannot fool all the people all the time'* should be attributed to him. After all, this was the man who calculated (conservatively) that *'There's a sucker born every minute.'* But it was actually Honest Abe Lincoln (q.v.) who most probably had the original handle on fooling the populace. In a campaign speech in Clinton, Illinois, in 1858, Lincoln supposedly made the remark, though direct evidence for this remains inconclusive.[39]

Bernard Baruch (1870–1965), stock-market genius, self-made multimillionaire and unpaid economic adviser to every US president from Woodrow Wilson to Jack F. Kennedy. History does not tell us if those presidents really wanted economic advice or stock-market tips.

Baruch told the South Carolina legislature on 16 April 1947: *'Let us not be deceived – we are today in the midst of a cold war.'* When he repeated the words before the Senate War

Investigating Committee on 24 October the next year, they were taken up by the nation's most influential political commentator, Walter Lippmann, and soon attributed to him. Not only were they not Lippmann's words, they weren't Baruch's either. They were suggested to him by Herbert Bayard Swope, the one-time editor of the *New York World* and three times Pulitzer Prize winner.[40]

Lord Beaverbrook (Sir [William] Maxwell Aitken Bt., 1st Baron), *see* Stanley Baldwin

The Venerable Bede, *see* the Bible

Mrs (Samuel) Beeton (née Isabella Mary Mayson, 1836–65), married a publisher and died after the birth of her fourth son.

Mrs Beeton's most famous phrase, '*First catch your hare*' does not appear in her most famous book *Mrs Beeton's Household Management* nor in any other of her works – which she probably didn't write anyway. In the five years between the publication of her *Household Management* (in parts, 1859–60) and her death, she published a great deal as well as having her wifely responsibilities. She must have been a great editor rather than a great writer. Nor was '*First catch your hare*' written by Hannah Glasse (possibly the pen-name of Dr John Hill, 1716–75, and possibly not).[41] In *The Art of Cookery Made Plain and Easy* (1747), her words are: 'Take your hare when it is cased and make a pudding . . .' Cased meant skinned rather than caught.[42] 'First catch your hare' is traditional, going back to at least the thirteenth century when it was known to Henry de Bracton (d. 1268).[43]

Hilaire Belloc (1870–1953), writer, poet and Roman

Catholic layman. Belloc, like Mark Twain (q.v.), only had to quote a remark to have it attributed to him, even when he gave a poetic footnote as attribution.

> *Like many of the Upper Class*
> *He liked the Sound of Broken Glass**[44]

Belloc's light verse is endlessly quotable. If you know *Matilda* and say 'Matilda told such Dreadful Lies', it is almost impossible to stop until you reach 'Matilda, and the House, were Burned', forty-eight lines later. Belloc also wrote . . .

> The accursed power which stands on Privilege
> (And goes with Women, and Champagne, and Bridge)
> Broke – and Democracy resumed her reign:
> (Which goes with Bridge, and Women, and Champagne)[45]

. . . but he did not write these double-edged lines which Fleet Street loves and sometimes attributes to him.

> *You cannot hope to bribe or twist*
> *Thank God! the British journalist.*
> *But, seeing what the man will do*
> *Unbribed, there's no occasion to.*[46]

They are by that underrated poet, the miniaturist Humbert Wolfe (1886–1940).

Saul Bellow (1915–), novelist, Pulitzer and Nobel Laureate

---

* 'A line I stole with subtle Daring, From Wing-Commander Maurice Baring.'

– which isn't enough to protect a man from those who know how the rest of us should think, and spend their time denouncing those who fail to meet their requirements.

Bellow, a Jew, has been criticized for ignoring the Holocaust *and* for defending the state of Israel. But his worst offence was to say *'When the Zulus produce* War and Peace *I'll take them seriously.'* His actual words were: 'The Papuans have had no Proust and the Zulus have not yet produced a Tolstoy.' When censured for telling the truth an unabashed Bellow replied: 'There's no Bulgarian Proust. Have I offended the Bulgarians too?'[47]

Robert Benchley, *see* Alexander Woollcott

Tom Berenger (b. 1950), the film actor, claims credit for the line usually attributed to George C. Scott. Ahead of a bedroom scene he said to the lady: 'Darling, if I get excited during this scene, please forgive me. And if I *don't* get excited please forgive me.'[48]

Lord Charles Beresford, *see* Marcel Proust

Ingrid Bergman, *see* Humphrey Bogart

Bernard of Chartres, *see* Isaac Newton

The Bible, in the King James's Authorized version, is so clearly, so memorably and so beautifully written that it has contributed more to the English language than any other single source. As a result it is seldom misquoted but there are some serious heresies.

Contrary to song and myth the animals did not all enter Noah's Ark *'two by two'*. Noah was instructed by God: 'Two of every living thing of all flesh, two of every sort shall thou bring into the ark, to keep them alive with thee; they shall be male and female.' Then God added: 'Of every clean beast thou shalt take to thee by sevens, the male and his female; and of beasts that are not clean by two, the male and the female. Of fowls also of the air by sevens, the male and the female: to keep seed alive upon the face of the earth.' The 'clean' beasts could be eaten (the others could not) or used for sacrifice; what the Royal Navy calls 'consumable stores'.[49]

Nor did the ark land on 'Mount Ararat' which would be difficult: mountains have steep sides. 'And the ark rested . . . upon the mountains of Ararat', an area, like 'the Peak District'.[50]

'Pride goeth before a fall.' Correctly, 'Pride goeth before destruction and a haughty spirit before a fall',[51] but John Heywood wrote elegantly: 'Pryde will have a fall. For pryde goeth before and shame cometh after.'[52]

'Spare the rod and spoil the child.' Two variations on this theme are offered by the book of Proverbs. 'He that spareth the rod hateth his child', and 'Foolishness is bound in the heart of a child; but the rod of correction shall drive it far from him.'[53] It was Samuel Butler (1612–80) in Hudibras who not only changed the wording to its best known form, but also put it into a different context.

> What medicine else can cure the fits
> Of lovers when they lose their wits?
> Love is a boy, by poets styled;
> Then spare the rod and spoil the child.[54]

Readers of the wrong class and generation may, like me, have learned the song which includes . . .

King Solomon and King David led wicked, wicked
  lives
With many, many concubines and many, many wives.
So when old age came on them, with many, many
  qualms
King Solomon wrote the Proverbs and King David
  wrote the Psalms.

. . . but the Proverbs are not by Solomon and the Psalms are not by David.[55]

'*Money is the root of all evil.*' In 1948 'The Money Song', with those words as the refrain,[56] was immensely popular with those who had too little money and with those who thought they had too little (*viz.*, everybody) and the assertion entered the English language. The original words are in St Paul's First Epistle to Timothy: '**The love of** money is the root of all evil.'[57] This is a double misquotation since biblical scholars are now agreed that Timothy was written by another hand. (Fundamentalists disagree – but does literal acceptance of whatever version of the Bible you adopt qualify as scholarship?)

The later Samuel Butler (1835–1902) developed the idea in *Erewhon*. 'It has been said that the love of money is the root of all evil. The want of money is so, quite as truly.'[58] Money itself – the purse of good but the heart of evil[59] – is neutral. In the same Epistle, St Paul is also credited with the term '*filthy lucre*'. 'A bishop then must be . . . not given to wine, no striker, not greedy of filthy lucre, but patient, not a brawler, not covetous.'[60] This was a mistranslation from the Greek by William Tyndale which was not corrected in the later King James Bible. As the ordinary person is indifferent to the metaphorical cleanliness of any money coming his way, 'filthy lucre' soon came to mean just 'money'.

Not '*There's safety in numbers*', but from Proverbs: 'Where no counsel is the people fall, but in the multitude of counsellors there is safety.'[61] That is an earlier version of 'Nobody ever got fired for buying IBM.' This was not because IBM computers, in their day, were more advanced, superior in performance and better value, but because the large number of people who bought IBM machines meant nobody could be criticized for doing so. In the late seventies professional fund managers in New York were all buying the same shares, the 'Nifty Fifty',[62] feeling that, so long as they were all wrong together, their jobs were safe even when their portfolios were not.

Not '*A merciful man is merciful unto his beast*', but '*A righteous man regardeth the life of his beast*',[63] and so does an unrighteous man if he has any commercial sense.

'*Fools rush in where angels fear to tread.*' Not the Bible but Alexander Pope (q.v.) in *An Essay on Criticism*.[64] The verse does not continue, as per the schoolboy legend, 'The angels are in heaven and all the fools are dead.'

'*Pouring oil on troubled waters*' is not the Bible but the Venerable Bede.[65]

The Bible is to be relied upon in all matters of animal husbandry so '*God tempers the wind to the shorn lamb*' is not biblical. Lambs are not shorn. Nor was the phrase first used by Maria in Sterne's *Sentimental Journey*. Maria distorted the sensible French proverb: '*Dieu mesure le froid à la brebis tondue*' – 'God measures the cold to the shorn sheep.'[66] (Sometimes *le vent*, the wind, rather than *le froid*.) When an author has a character make a characteristic mistake it is usually assumed the author is ignorant, lazy or incompetent – or all three. P. G. Wodehouse gave the working-class barmaid in one of his novels suitably colloquial habits of speech. His publisher's proofreader carefully corrected all the errors of grammar and syntax.

'*In the midst of life we are in death*' occurs not in the Bible but in the Book of Common Prayer.

One phrase which few would attribute to the Bible is '*And I escaped by the skin of my teeth*', but you will find it in the book of Job, although the 'by' is correctly 'with'.[67]

While some obsessives claim that the works of Shakespeare were written by someone else (Francis Bacon (q.v.) is favourite), they neglect the evidence that Shakespeare wrote the King James's Authorized version of the Bible. 'Shake' is the forty-sixth word of the forty-sixth psalm, and 'spear' is the forty-sixth word from the end of that psalm, while the book was published when Shakespeare was forty-six years old. Men have been hanged on slimmer evidence. *See also* The Golden Rule, Woodrow Wilson *and* Rabbi Phineas Ben Yair.

'F. E.' Smith, 1st Earl of Birkenhead (1872–1930), lawyer and politician. When there was talk of ousting the Conservative Party leader, Stanley Baldwin, in favour of Sir Robert Horne, he said: '*Why swop donkeys in mid-stream?*'

This abbreviates the story told by F.E.'s friend, Francis Hirst. 'When the Tory Party was troubled about the leadership on the eve of a general election [in 1929], he warned them against swopping donkeys in mid-stream. On that occasion I came across him in St James's Park. Taking my arm he said, in "strict confidence", that he had been to the Party headquarters and had advised them there was only one way of averting disaster. They should make a bid for the womens' vote by promising that, if returned to power, they would make Lucy [Baldwin] prime minister instead of Stanley.'[68]

Birkenhead did not admire qualities he lacked himself. 'We have the highest authority for believing that the meek shall inherit the earth; though I never have found any particular corroboration of this aphorism in the records [of Wills] at Somerset House.'[69] There are many stories of Birkenhead's wit, some of them true: for example, an aged crone shouted at a Liverpool election meeting: 'F. E. Smith, you're a bastard' to which he replied in a sorrowful tone: 'I told you not to come here . . . Mother.'

John Bidlake, *see* Alfred Austin

Prince Otto von Bismarck, *see* R. A. Butler

Humphrey Bogart (1899–1957), American film actor. Some people who know the request *'Play it again, Sam'*, also know that Rick, Bogart's character in *Casablanca* (1942), never uttered the famous imperative but that Ilse Lund (Ingrid Bergman) made the request of the pianist. Few of them know that she actually said 'Play it, Sam. Play *As Time Goes By*.' Mr Bogart then rather rudely interjects, 'If she can stand it I can. Play it!' Woody Allen used the phrase for the title of his stage play and feature film, *Play It Again, Sam*. The scriptwriters of *Casablanca*, Julius J. Epstein, Philip G. Epstein and Howard Koch must also be credited for the equally classic and more accurately quoted, 'Here's looking at you, kid.'[70]

Bogart himself said: 'Contrary to legend, as a juvenile I never said *"Tennis, anyone?"* just as I never said *"Drop the gun, Loui"* as a heavy.'[71] The line 'Anyone for a game of tennis?' occurs in Bernard Shaw's play *Misalliance* (1914) and I cannot trace an earlier usage.

Lady Violet Bonham-Carter, *see* David Lloyd George

Napoleon Bonaparte, *see* Napoleon

Borgia family, *see* Graham Greene

Horatio Bottomley (1860–1933), self-made millionaire, bankrupt, journalist, orator, Member of Parliament, confidence trickster and jailbird.

There is no better example of Dr Samuel Johnson's reflection, 'Patriotism is the last refuge of a scoundrel' (q.v.). In 1906 Bottomley founded the ultra-patriotic *John Bull* magazine which made special offers to readers in order to defraud them. During the Great War he toured the country selling Victory Bonds, but most of the money ended up in his pocket, not the government's. Sentenced to seven years imprisonment in 1919, he was seen by a visiting friend sewing mailbags – then the main occupation for guests of His Majesty. '*Ah, Bottomley, sewing?*' '*No, reaping*', came the reply.[72] Since visitors were not allowed into prison workshops Bottomley, whose sense of humour remained intact, is the probable author of this pleasing invention. (A less elegant variation has Bottomley in the prison garden, actually 'sowing'.)

Charles Boyer (1897–1978), the romantic French actor, played romantic French heroes with romantic French accents in romantic American films.

One such film was *Algiers* (1938), co-starring Hedy Lamarr, none of which was shot closer to Algeria than Hollywood. A thousand impersonators have since said '*Come wiz me to ze kasbah*', but Boyer never utters the line in the film, nor anywhere else. It was, as usual, made up by a press agent.[73]

Mrs Bessie Braddock MP, *see* Winston L. S. Churchill

Marlon Brando (1924–), has often been heard to say: '*An actor is a kind of guy who if you ain't talking about him ain't listening*', but he is only quoting George Glass.[74]

John Bright (1811–89), Britain's great nineteenth-century radical, coined the phrase '*England is the Mother of Parliaments*' when speaking in Birmingham Town Hall on 18 January 1865. But he was not, as is unanimously believed in the House of Commons, crediting the House of Commons nor even the two Houses of Parliament with imposing Westminster-style parliaments on countries thoroughly unsuited to them. When Bright talked of 'parliaments' he meant the sequence of Parliaments that met at Westminster, the life of one parliament being from its election to its dissolution.

Drew 'Bundini' Brown, *see* Muhammad Ali

Edmund Burke (1729–97), politician, political theorist and pioneer democrat. He is known for '*The only thing necessary for evil to triumph is for good men to do nothing.*' The closest in Burke's writing is: 'When bad men combine, the good must associate; else they will fall, one by one, an unpitied sacrifice, in a contemptible struggle.'

In moving his 'Resolution For Conciliation With the [American] Colonies' in the House of Commons on 22 March 1775, Burke declaimed: 'I do not know the method of drawing up an indictment against an whole people', but this was soon trimmed to the apophthegm '*You cannot indict a whole people.*' This is a rare example of the popular paraphrase remaining faithful to the original remark.

Truth may, or may not be stranger than fiction, but neither assertion can be an absolute. Burke was too wise to say '*Truth is stranger than fiction*', which is an out-of-context mangling of 'Fiction lags after truth': in context, 'When we speak of commerce with our [American] colonies, fiction lags after truth; invention is unfruitful and imagination cold and barren.'[75] Lord Byron wrote: "Tis strange but true; for truth is always strange – Stranger than fiction',[76] but then poets are allowed greater licence than lesser wordsmiths.

Members of the press are fond of quoting Edmund Burke's dramatic gesture in the Commons when, pointing to the reporters, he declared: *'There are Three Estates in Parliament; but in the Reporters' Gallery yonder, there sits a Fourth Estate more important by far than they all'*, as reported by Thomas Carlyle,[77] who was, unconsciously, quoting Thomas Babington Macaulay (q.v.): 'The Gallery in which the reporters sit has become a fourth estate of the realm', writing in 1828.[78] I prefer Carlyle's version, even though it cannot be found in Burke's writing or speeches. (The Three Estates of the Realm are the Lords Spiritual, the Lords Temporal and the Members of the House of Commons.)

Burke was a great democrat but he wasn't bigoted about it. He is the man who first called urban mobs 'the great unwashed'.[79] In this century the insecure middle class used 'the unwashed' as a semi-code word for the lower orders. The phrase also became a term of abuse in America with the *Congressional Record* noting in 1901: 'The Democratic Party has long been known as "the great unwashed".'[80] However both John Gay (1685–1732) and Shakespeare recorded earlier uses of 'unwashed' as a pejorative against the lower orders.[81] *See also* Sir Robert Armstrong *and* Alexander Pope.

Edgar Rice Burroughs (1875–1950), wrote the *Tarzan* novellas, beginning with *Tarzan of the Apes* in 1914. There were many silent films of *Tarzan*, but the first of the *Tarzan* talkies was *Tarzan the Ape Man* made in 1932 starring

Johnny Weissmuller and Maureen O'Sullivan. Mr Weissmuller said: 'I didn't have to act in *Tarzan the Ape Man* – just say *"Me Tarzan, you Jane."*'[82] This examplar of the movie promptly became Tarzan's best remembered, indeed only remembered, line, but it was not said by Tarzan in any of the *Tarzan* books or films, only by Mr Weissmuller.

Robert Burton, *see* Edward Bulwer Lytton, Sir Isaac Newton and Proverbial

R. A. ('RAB') Butler (Lord Butler of Saffron Walden, 1902–82), statesman.

Butler, like Sir Geoffrey Howe, proves that in a modern democracy the qualities needed to become prime minister are different to, and incompatible with, those needed to do the job well. Sir Anthony Eden had the former but not the latter. Butler is credited with calling him *'the best prime minister we have'*, a remark to savour. But the credit belongs to the journalist who asked Butler, 'Would you say he is the best prime minister we have?' To this Butler replied only 'Yes', which is not much of a quote on its own. Lord Butler reflected: 'My hurried assent to this well meant but meaningless proposition was flashed round the world; indeed it was fathered on me. I do not think it did Anthony any good. It did not do me any good either.'[83] When Butler, who failed to succeed Eden to the premiership, also failed to succeed Macmillan, the gag was neatly reversed and he became 'the best prime minister we never had'.[84]

In his autobiography Butler wrote: 'Politics is the *art of the possible*. That is what these pages show I have tried to achieve – not more – and that is what I have called my book',[85] and popular misconception has ever since credited him with authorship of the phrase. In fact it can be traced back at least as far as the Great Prussian chancellor, Otto von Bismarck. He used it when talking to Meyer von Waldeck on 11 August 1867, saying *'Die Politik ist die Lehre vom Moglichen'*, or 'Politics is the art of the possible.' And, while on Bismarck, Sidney Whitman wrote: 'I may avail myself of the opportunity of denying once more the truth of the story that Prince Bismarck had ever likened Lord Salisbury to a lath of wood painted to look like iron.'[86] The assertion of anyone using 'may' in so ugly and incorrect a fashion is not to be trusted. The remark is in character with the Iron Chancellor and has just enough truth in it to sting.

Samuel Butler (1612–80), author of *Hudibras*. Butler's 'To swallow gudgeons ere th'are catched/And count their chickens ere th'are hatched', is pleasingly more elegant than *'Don't count your chickens till they're hatched'* – but ours is an impatient age with little time for subtlety or style.

Similarly deft is Butler's 'For those that fly may fight again/Which he can never do that's slain' – and how much more quotable than the later, longer, better known:

> For he that fights and runs away
> May live to fight another day
> But he who is in battle slain
> Will never rise to fight again.

. . . which is the popular corruption from Ray's eighteenth-century original,[87] which is only quoting Desiderius Erasmus (?1466–1536), 'He that fights and runs away may live to fight another day.'[88] Scholars, not being warriors, have always had a soft spot for cowards, but have usually been too craven to admit to it. *See also* the Bible.

Samuel Butler (1835–1902), author of *Erewhon*. *See* the Bible.

John Byrom, *see* Lewis Carroll

George Gordon, Lord Byron (1788–1824), English poet and Greek hero. The man whose looks gave birth to the adjective 'Byronic'.

Lord Byron is often credited with the one-liner much loved by authors '*Now Barabbas was a publisher*', from St John's Gospel 'Now Barabbas was a robber.' It was not his line but that of the poet Thomas Campbell (1777–1844)[89] who, during the Napoleonic Wars, proposed a toast at an authors' dinner 'to Napoleon'. But scarcely had he said the word than murmurs of dissent were heard. 'I agree with you that Napoleon is a tyrant, a monster, the sworn foe of our nation. But gentlemen – he once shot a publisher.' (A German, Johann Phillip Palm, was put to death in August 1806 on Napoleon's orders for printing and publishing seditious pamphlets.) Norman Douglas, author of *South Wind*, summed up the feeling of authors. 'It is with publishers as with wives: one always wants somebody else's.'[90]

Good-mannered reticence is not usual in books of quotations.* Nevertheless, all those on my shelves tactfully omit '*See Naples and die.*' The Neapolitans will tell you that when the Greeks established their city as Neapolis (new city) it was the most beautiful place in all the world and the correct saying is '*See Naples, then die*', because life will have nothing more to offer you.[91] Which is what you would expect them to say. The tourist boards of other Mediterranean

---

* Least of all in this one.

states will, no doubt, point out that in the eighteenth and nineteenth centuries the visitor to Naples was as likely to die of typhoid and cholera as to return home – and that in the twentieth century Naples remains one of the most crime-ridden cities in Europe. Which is also what you would expect them to say. The only certainty is that Byron never coined the remark, in spite of it often being attributed to him. *See also* Edmund Burke, Winston L. S. Churchill, John Milton *and* La Marquise de Sévigné.

C

James Cagney (1896–1986), American film actor. The bread-and-butter line of every aspiring impersonator, Cagney's famous tag *'You dirty rat!'* was never said by the star in any of his seventy-plus films. Or so the actor claimed.[92] Neither were the variations *'You dirty rats!'* or *'Yous dirty rats!'* But in the otherwise forgettable gangster film *Blonde Crazy* (1931), Mr Cagney's character does refer to one of his fictional cohorts as: 'You dirty, double-crossing rat.'[93]

(Leonard) James Callaghan (Lord Callaghan of Cardiff, 1912–) British Prime Minister 1976–9.

Which of us would not enjoy a break in sunny Guadeloupe, staying at the best hotel, in the middle of winter and all at someone else's expense? British premier James Callaghan and his Chancellor of the Exchequer, Denis Healey, enjoyed such a break, and had the excuse of a summit meeting to do so – although nobody can recall offhand what the 1979 Guadeloupe meeting was about and what it achieved, if anything. Callaghan arrived back at Heathrow to a Britain beset by industrial strife and economic problems. When asked about these, a badly briefed 'Sunny Jim' Callaghan did not reply *'Crisis? What Crisis?'*. That was merely the *Sun*'s parody of what he did say. 'I don't think other people in the world would share the view that there is a mounting crisis.'[94] Politicians can survive almost anything except ridicule, and Callaghan lost the general election later that year.

Pierre, Baron de Cambronne (1770–1842), an officer of the Napoleonic Guard at the Battle of Waterloo, was called upon to surrender. *'The Guards die but never surrender'* (*'La Guarde meurt mais ne se rend pas'*) was his valiant reply.

As de Cambronne lived for another twenty-seven years, the story has at least one exception to test the rule. At a banquet in his home town of Nantes in 1830 he vehemently denied uttering the words, but the city fathers, no more willing to spoil a good story than anyone else, still put them on the statue of de Cambronne they erected after his death.[95] The scene had been situation comedy. Upon Colonel Halkett calling on de Cambronne to surrender, he said *'Merde'** and surrendered. De Cambronne's valiant heroic '. . . was concocted by Balisson de Rougemont, a prolific author of *mots*, two days after the battle, in the *Independant'*.[96]

Thomas Campbell, *see* Lord Byron *and* George Morris

King Canute (or Cnut), *see* Francis Bacon

---

* Which you don't need translated. *'Merde'* is still known as *'Le mot de Cambronne'* in France.

Capitalists Misquoting Communists For seven decades the world was distracted by the battle of ideas between capitalism and communism – both of which meant different things to different people. The communist ideal was the more noble and nonsensical; capitalist economics those which actually work. It was always obvious to pyschologists and market economists that capitalism would win the day – but none could predict when. As early as 1927 Will Rogers said: 'Communism is like prohibition, it's a good idea but it won't work.'[97] During those seventy years both sides misquoted each other furiously. The following is a sample of fake quotes put into the mouths of communists, mainly to try and frighten Middle America.[98]

Lavrenti Beria (1899–1958) did not say: *'By psycho-politics create chaos. Leave a nation leadlerless. Kill our enemies. And bring to earth through communism the greatest peace man has ever known.'*

Leonid Brezhnev (1906–82) did not say: *'Our aim is to gain control of the two great treasure-houses on which the West depends ... The energy treasure-house of the Persian Gulf and the mineral treasure-house of Central and Southern Africa.'*

Gus Hall (1910–), General Secretary of the American Communist Party, did not say: *'I dream of the hour when the last Congressman is strangled to death on the guts of the last preacher.'*

Nikita Khrushchev (1884–1971) did not say: *'We cannot expect the Americans to jump from capitalism to communism, but we can aid their elected leaders in giving* *them small doses of socialism until they suddenly awake to find they have Communism.'*

Josef Stalin (Yosef Vissarionovich Dzhugashvili, 1879–1953) did not say: *'Take Eastern Europe, the masses of Asia, surround the US by taking Africa, Central and South America and we will not have to fight for it. It [America] will fall into our hands like a ripe fruit.'*

Zhou Enlai (1888–1976) did not say: *'If you want to help the Vietnamese you should encourage the Americans to throw more and more soldiers into Vietnam. We are planting the best kind of opium especially for the American soldiers in Vietnam.'*

See also Sir Edward Heath, Lenin *and* Gregoriy Zinoviev. For examples of misquoted capitalists *see* Charles de Gaulle, Henry Kissinger, Ronald Reagan *and* Franklin D. Roosevelt.

Truman Capote, *see* Her Grace the Duchess of Windsor

Thomas Carlyle (1795–1881), British writer and historian. *'Genius is an infinite capacity for taking pains.'* Carlyle is generally credited with this pithy observation, but it is derived from his biography of Frederick the Great in a form a little less compact and neat: 'The good plan itself, this comes not of its own accord; it is the fruit of genius (which means transcendent capacity of taking trouble, first of all . . .).' After devoting fourteen years and six volumes to Frederick's life, Mr Carlyle should know.[99] *See also* Edmund Burke.

Lewis Carroll (Revd Charles Lutwidge Dodgson, 1832–98),

was a lecturer in mathematics at Christ Church, Oxford, but famous as the author of *Alice in Wonderland* and *Alice through the Looking Glass*. Queen Victoria was entranced by the *Alice* books and asked for further works by the same author. She was sent *Euclid And His Modern Rivals* (1879). Carroll wrote . . .

> Tweedledum and Tweedledee
> Agreed to have a battle;
> For Tweedledum said Tweedledee
> Had spoilt his nice new rattle

. . . and was credited with inventing those unterrifying twins. Musicians know better, or used to. In the early eighteenth century there was great rivalry between two expatriate London composers with most of the Court and aristocracy taking sides.

> Some say compared to Bonconcini
> That mynheer Handel's but a ninny;
> Others aver that he to Handel
> Is scarcely fit to hold a candle.
> Strange all this difference should be
> Twixt Tweedledum and Tweedledee.

The verse is probably John Byrom's, although Swift and Pope have also been credited with it. To 'tweedle' is to produce a succession of shrill musical sounds, to whistle or pipe. 'Tweedledum' and 'Tweedledee' were used to suggest the contrast between the sounds of high and low pitched instruments. Handel became one of the world's great composers; Bonconcini became so little regarded that he did not even achieve a modest entry in the massive 1911 edition of

Encyclopaedia Britannica. Now he is only remembered for Byrom's doggerel.

Carroll immortalized the grin of the Cheshire Cat but the phrase is certainly much older because, Brewer assures us, 'cheese was formerly sold in Cheshire moulded like a cat'. He fails to tell us why. John Wolcot writing as Peter Pindar used the phrase in the eighteenth century.[100] *See also* Sir Hartley Shawcross.

'Jimmy' (James Earl) Carter, *see* Sir Robert Armstrong *and* Lyndon Baines Johnson

Dame Barbara Cartland, *see* HRH Charles, Prince of Wales

Mr Justice Caulfield (1914–), a High Court Judge, and in private life Sir Bernard Caulfield.

When an elderly judge goes absolutely doolally over an enchanting young witness it gives a welcome boost to the cause of public entertainment. It was Mr Justice Caulfield who gave new life to the word 'fragrant' when referring to Mary Archer, wife of the best-selling author Jeffrey who was then suing the *Star*, one of Britain's irrepressible tabloid papers, for libel. Mr Justice Caulfield did not, as everyone believes, call Mrs Archer *'fragrant'*; he was too wily for that. Instead he put the matter to the jury thus. 'Remember Mary Archer in the witness box. Your vision of her will probably never disappear. Has she elegance? Has she fragrance? Would she have – without the strain of this trial – a radiance?' All of which helped her husband, now the Rt. Hon. Lord Archer of Weston-super-Mare in the County of Somerset, win £500,000 in damages – tax free.[101]

Caesarius, Bishop of Arles, *see* Athanasius

Lord Hugh Cecil (later 1st Baron Quickswood, 1868–1956), youngest son of the 3rd Marquess of Salisbury, politician and Anglican churchman.

It was Lord Hugh who said of prime minister Neville Chamberlain 'He is no better than a mayor of Birmingham – and in a lean year at that',[102] which is usually credited to Winston Churchill or David Lloyd George, both of whom said of Chamberlain: 'He saw foreign policy through the wrong end of a municipal drainpipe', but no record shows who said it first.

(Arthur) Neville Chamberlain, *see* Francis I

King Charles II, *see* Samuel Pepys

Charles V of France *see* Francis I

Charles, Prince of Prussia, *see* Colonel William Prescott

Charles, Prince of Wales (His Royal Highness Charles Philip Arthur George, KG, KT, GCB, AK, QSO, PC, ADC, Prince of Wales and Earl of Chester, Duke of Cornwall, Duke of Rothsay, Earl of Carrick and Baron Renfrew, Lord of The Isles and Great Steward of Scotland, 1948–).

In a speech to the Royal Institute of British Architects in 1984, Prince Charles made the rather startling announcement, 'I would understand better this type of high-tech approach if you demolished the whole of Trafalgar Square and started again', and then continued, '... *but what is proposed is like a monstrous carbuncle on the face of a much loved and elegant friend.*'[103] Thus Charles the Architectural Critic (or Philistine, depending on your views) was born.

But it was his then stepmother-in-law, Countess Spencer, who was the originator of this striking simile. In the charming travelogue *The Spencers on Spas* (he of the photos, she of the captions) she writes: 'Alas, for our towns and cities. Monstrous carbuncles of concrete have erupted in gentle Georgian squares.'[104] There are claims that the phrase's true origin is to be found somewhere among the hundreds of novels of Dame Barbara Cartland. But these remain unsubstantiated.

Geoffrey Chaucer, *see* William Shakespeare

Earl of Chesterfield, [105] *see* Duke of Wellington

Winston L. S. Churchill (from 1953 Sir Winston, 1874–1965), British politician, prime minister 1940–45 and 1951–5. Churchill was addicted to making remarks which were then plagiarized by earlier generations.

Churchill was the master of the understated put-down. After being defeated in the 1945 general election he called the new Labour prime minister, Clement Attlee, '*a sheep in sheep's clothing*'. Two years earlier F. Greenslet published *Under The Bridge*. 'At a lunch given by Edmund Gosse (*c.* 1906) . . . the woolly-bearded poet Sturge Moore entered late . . . Gosse, a naughty host, whispered in my ear: "A sheep in sheep's clothing."'[106]

Another Churchill jibe at Attlee was: 'An empty taxi drew up outside 10 Downing Street and Mr Attlee got out', but Churchill denied the quote. 'Mr Attlee is an honourable and gallant gentleman, and a faithful colleague who has served his country well at the time of its greatest need . . . I should never make such a remark about him and I strongly disapprove of anyone who does.' Major Attlee survived service in Gallipoli, Churchill's disastrous Great War campaign when over half the Allied troops died.

Churchill said of Sir Stafford Cripps, Labour's ascetic and puritan Chancellor of the Exchequer (1947–50), '*There but for the grace of God, goes God.*' This was said, and widely reported, by Herman Mankiewicz of Orson Welles, when the two were writing the script of *Citizen Kane* in 1940.[107] A sixteenth-century Englishman, Revd John Bradford, upon seeing convicts taken away for execution said thankfully: 'But for the grace of God there goes John Bradford.'[108] The irony is that Bradford was burned at the stake as a heretic in 1555.

Churchill voiced one of his most famous phrases, '*an iron curtain*', when speaking at Fulton College, Missouri, on 5 March 1946. He said 'From Stettin in the Baltic, to Trieste in the Adriatic, an iron curtain has descended across the continent.' The American author St Vincent Troubridge used the Fulton aphorism five months earlier on 21 October 1945: 'There is an iron curtain across Europe', in the *Sunday Empire News*. Hitler's propaganda minister, Joseph Goebbels, also used the term on 25 February that year in *Das Reich*. In 1920 Ethel Snowden (wife of Philip Snowden, Labour first Chancellor of the Exchequer in 1923), used the phrase in her book published that year, *Through Bolshevik Russia* where she exclaims: 'We were behind the "iron curtain" at last.' In 1914 the queen of the Belgians spoke of 'a bloody iron curtain' between her and the Germans. The earliest use of the description is found in the Earl of Munster's journal of 1817.[109]

Among Churchill's most famous sentences is one from his speech to the House of Commons on 13 May 1940, his first after becoming prime minister. '*I have nothing to offer but blood, toil, sweat and tears*', but anyone who quotes the original words is likely to be 'corrected'. They were: 'I have nothing to offer but blood and toil, tears and sweat.' An almost identical sentence occurs in Henry James's 1886 novel *The Bostonians*, but Churchill claimed never to have read the book and to have coined the words himself.

Churchill suggested to President Franklin D. Roosevelt that the successor body to the discredited League of Nations should be the *United Nations*, which F. D. R. enthusiastically accepted. Churchill took the line from Lord Byron.

> Millions of tongues record thee, and anew
> Their children's lips shall echo them and say –
> 'Here, where the sword **united nations** drew
> Our countrymen were warring on that day!'
> And this is much, and all which will not pass away.[110]

There is a famous anecdote about Churchill and Bessie Braddock, the broad-beamed Labour MP for the Exchange division of Liverpool. This story is usually told shorn of all Churchill's wit, Augustan English and the unlikely friendship between the two. Correctly it goes:

B. B., reprovingly: 'Winston. You're drunk, you're very drunk.'

W. S. C., cheerfully: 'Bessie, you're fat, you're very fat – and the difference between us is that I shall be sober in the morning.'

Mrs Braddock lived in Zigzag Road.

Hoi polloi are inclined to credit any remark about cigars to Churchill, but he did not even claim to have said '*A woman is only a woman, but a good cigar is a smoke.*' Nor is P. G. Wodehouse the author, although he once wrote a short story, *A Good Cigar Is A Smoke*: he was quoting his friend

Rudyard Kipling who coined the line.[111] *See also* Benito Mussolini, The Oxford Union, Ronald W. Reagan, Sir Hartley Shawcross *and* Lord Hugh Cecil.

Arthur Christiansen, *see* Sir Robert Armstrong

Count Ciano, *see* John F. Kennedy

Colley Cibber, *see* William Shakespeare

Marcus Tullius Cicero (sometimes called simply 'Tully', 106–43 BC). In a trenchant article of 15 January 1986 headed 'We'll Never Learn', the *Kansas City Star* quoted the ancient wisdom of the Roman orator, writer and statesman. *'The budget should be balanced. The Treasury should be filled. Public debt should be reduced. The arrogance of officials should be tempered and controlled, and assistance to foreign lands should be curtailed lest we ourselves should become bankrupt. The people should be forced to work and not depend upon government subsistence.'*

Cicero was not the proto-Reaganite those policies indicate as the quotation can only be traced back to 15 January 1986. The counterfeiter's economics may have been sound but not his, or her, sociology. How many readers of the *Kansas City Star*, I wonder, spend their leisure moments browsing through *De Natura Deorum* or *De Senectute?* (Or, for that matter, the readers of the *Kensington Post?*) *See also* Voltaire.

General Karl von Clausewitz (1780–1831), Prussian officer and author of *Vom Kreige*, (On War) 1832.

Von Clausewitz is usually credited with: *'I divide officers into four classes; the lazy, the stupid, the clever and the industrious. Each officer possesses at least two of these qualities. Those who are clever and industrious are fitted for high staff appointments. Use* can be made of those who are stupid and lazy. The man who is clever and lazy is fit for the very highest command. He has the temperament and the requisite nerves to deal with all situations. But whoever is stupid and industrious must be removed immediately.'[112] Lt.-Col. Norman Murphy worked diligently to track down this quotation, finding it attributed to many other officers as well as von Clausewitz. But he could find no trace of it before its use by General Kurt von Hammerstein[113] in 1933. Nobody ever attributes this apophthegm to American or English generals.

Naturally von Clausewitz's most famous phrase, 'War is the continuation of politics by others means', was neatly summarized from the original so as to lose a crucial part of its meaning. 'War is nothing but the continuation of politics with the admixture of other means.' ('Der Krieg ist nichts als eine Fortsetsung des politischen Vekehrs mit Einmischung anderer Mittel.') Zhou Enlai, when Chinese foreign minister in 1954, said: 'All diplomacy is a continuation of war by other means', while his leader, Mao Zedong, said: 'Politics is war without bloodshed while war is politics with bloodshed.'[114]

Cassius Clay Jr., *see* Muhammad Ali

Clinton, William Jefferson, *see* Muhammad Ali

Samuel Langhorne Clemens, *see* Mark Twain

Claud Cockburn (1904–81), anarchic socialist and wit, was a sub-editor on *The Times* in the thirties, when such posts were competed for by Oxbridge graduates with first-class degrees. In those happy days one error of spelling, grammar or syntax in the paper would result in a post-mortem the next morning chaired by the editor himself. Cockburn claims, in his autobiography *In Times Of Trouble*, to have won a competition among his peers for the most boring headline in the paper with his entry: '*Small Earthquake in Chile. Not Many Dead.*'[115] Some humourless souls went in search of the headline in the back numbers of *The Times*, and were disappointed when it was not there. Mr Cockburn had a sense of humour.

George M. Cohan (1878–1942), entertainer closely associated with New York's Broadway theatreland.

The sentiment '*It doesn't matter what they say as long as they spell the name right*' is odd. All civilized societies have laws of libel just because it **does** matter what they – usually the press – say, especially when they spell the name right. However a publicity-averse recluse is less likely to have his aphorisms in lexica of quotations than, say, George M. Cohan. 'I don't care what you say about me, as long as you say something about me, and as long as you spell my name right.'[116] The maxim has been attributed to President Roosevelt, although nobody seems sure which one. In 1985 David Owen, then leader of the Social Democrats, said desperately: 'I don't care if you criticize us, agree with us or disagree with us. Just mention us, that is all we ask.'[117] John Wolcot (1738–1819), writing as Peter Pindar, expressed it better and first.

> What rage for fame attends both great and small!
> Better be damned than mentioned not at all.[118]

Charles Caleb Colton, *see* John Milton

Communism, *see* Capitalism

Confucius, *see* Anon. *and* The Golden Rule

William Congreve (1670–1729), dramatist and poet. In his tragedy *The Mourning Bride* (1697) Congreve notes that 'Music hath charms to soothe a savage breast/To soften rocks, or bend a knotted oak', which is a far cry from the more famous and dubious observation that *'Music hath charms to soothe the savage beast.'*

The now politically incorrect truism that *'Hell hath no fury like a woman scorned'*, is also derived from the same play. The original dialogue reads, 'Heav'n has no rage, like love to hatred turn'd. Nor Hell a fury, like a woman scorn'd.'[119]

This aphorism has spawned more children than a sultan's harem. Frank Sinatra gave the idea a typically American twist: 'Hell hath no fury like a hustler with a literary agent.'[120] The journalist Charles Montague, having served in the Great War, said: 'War hath no fury like a non-combatant.' My favourites, by Anon., are the twins: 'Hell hath no fury like an unpunctual person kept waiting', and 'Hell hath no fury like an habitual liar disbelieved when telling the truth.'

A. J. (Arthur) Cook (1884–1932), Secretary of the Miners' Federation at the time of the General Strike in 1926. This self-proclaimed 'humble follower of Lenin' has the distinction of misquoting himself. Ahead of the Strike, he coined as the miners' rallying cry the somewhat abrupt: 'Not a cent off. Not a second on.'[121] This was then worked upon, and in a speech in York on 3 April 1926 it blossomed into its famous doggerel form, *'Not a penny off the pay. Not a second on the day.'*[122]

(John) Calvin Coolidge *(1872–1933). The taciturnity of

---

* It is curious how many politicans do not use their first given name. Of British prime ministers in this century alone, they are: (Herbert Henry) Asquith, (Andrew) Bonar Law, (James) Ramsay MacDonald, (Arthur) Neville

America's thirtieth president (1923–9) became legendary. 'I have noticed that nothing I never said ever did me any harm.'[123] Washington wits and the press corps vied in inventing new examples of Coolidge's short way with words. A genuine Coolidge story was of the telegram sent to Samuel Gompers, president of the American Federation of Labor, on 14 September 1919 when the Boston police went on strike: 'There is no right to strike against the public safety by anybody, anywhere, anytime',[124] which couldn't be better put.

In 1922 when the British were renegotiating their war debts, Coolidge did not say, *'They hired the money, didn't they?'* although his widow said it was the sort of judgement he might have made, as she did of another apocryphal anecdote. *Mrs Coolidge, unable to go to church one Sunday, asked the President what the sermon was about. 'Sin,' came the reply. 'Well. What did he say about sin?' 'He was against it.'*[125]

He did not say *'The business of America is business'*, but the more balanced: 'The chief business of the American people is business.'[126]

He may have looked '. . . *as if he had been weaned on a pickle*', but Alice Roosevelt Longworth (q.v., the acerbic daughter of President Theodore Roosevelt) didn't say so; she quoted her dentist who had it from a previous victim.[127] *See also* Wilson Mizner, Dorothy Parker *and* Alexander Woollcott.

(Alfred) Duff Cooper (1st Viscount Norwich), *see Private Eye*

Chamberlain, (Robert) Anthony Eden, (Maurice) Harold Hacmillan, (James) Harold Wilson and (Leonard) James Callaghan.

Denise Cordelier, *see* William Shakespeare

Pierre Corneille, *see* John Milton

Anne-Marie Corneul, *see* La Marquise de Sévigné

Sir Noel Coward (1899–1973), playwright, lyricist, composer, actor, author. Asked the secret of acting, Sir Noel replied: *'Know your lines, speak up and don't bump into the furniture'*, but this is a traditional actors' joke (if it is a joke). *See also* Spencer Tracy.

Michael Crawford (1942–), the British actor, has adorned every part he has played, but remains in the hearts of the British public for his role as Frank Spencer in *Some Mothers Do 'Ave 'Em* (1974–9). The line, originally *Don't Some Mothers 'Ave 'Em*, was the catch-phrase of the Lancashire comedian, Jimmy Clitheroe, taken from his long-running radio show of the fifties, *The Clitheroe Kid*.

Sir Edward Creasy, *see* The Duke of Wellington

Oliver Cromwell (1599–1658), regicide. It says much about this Puritan general that he did not instruct his troops, about to cross a river, *'Put your trust in God and keep your powder dry'*, but 'Put your trust in God **but mind** to keep your powder dry.'[128] The extra emphasis of 'but mind' reveals a man with more faith in precautions than in prayer. Cromwell wrote to the elders of the Church of Scotland: 'I beseech you, in the bowels of Christ, think it possible you may be mistaken', but it never occurred to him that possibly he might be mistaken.[129]

Sellar and Yeatman summed up the Civil War succinctly

in *1066 And All That*: 'The utterly memorable Struggle between the Cavaliers (Wrong but Wromantic) and the Roundheads (Right but Repulsive).'[130] *See also* Napoleon Bonaparte.

Frank Crowninshield, *see* Gertrude Stein

John Curran, *see* Thomas Jefferson

George Curzon, Marquess Curzon of Keddleston (1859–1925), former Viceroy of India and later foreign secretary.

Lord Curzon was visiting troops behind the lines in Flanders during the Great War. Upon seeing soldiers bathing in the vats of an abandoned brewery he was quoted as exclaiming: *'I had no conception that the lower orders had such white skins.'* Lord Curzon's reputation as an aristocrat 'acutely aware of the existence of class distinctions' ensured this attribution stuck. There is no evidence he ever had such thoughts, let alone voiced them, but as one biographer, Harold Nicolson, wrote: 'Curzon would deny the authenticity of this story, but loved it none the less.'[131]

D

Charles Darwin (1809–82), scientist and author. Darwin discovered the principles of natural and sexual selection, but is also responsible for, at least indirectly, the bugbears of 'creation science' and social Darwinism. His writings and theories have always been subject to distortions and mis-interpretations, from their first publication to the present day.

The most dramatic fabrication has to be an account of Darwin's final words which, according to a certain Lady Hope (conspicuously not present), were: *'How I wish I had not expressed my theory of evolution as I have done.'* Refuted by his family, this recantation of his life's work continues to be used as ammunition by fundamentalists and evangelicals in their crusades against secular humanism.

Nor did Darwin coin 'survival of the fittest'. As he wrote: 'The expression often used by Mr Herbert Spencer of the survival of the fittest is more accurate and sometimes more convenient.' Spencer himself wrote in *Principles of Biology* (1865), 'It cannot but happen ... that those will survive whose functions happen to be most nearly in equilibrium with the modified aggregate of external forces ... This survival of the fittest implies multiplication of the fittest.' The thought was best expressed by Robert Service (1874–1958).

This is the Law of the Yukon, that only the strong shall thrive
That surely the weak shall perish, and only the fit survive.

This has the added convenience that, in place of 'the Yukon', you can substitute 'Wall Street' or 'business' or 'the suburbs' *et cetera* and the lines still scan and remain true.

In another of Spencer's works, this true (if unwitting) architect of social Darwinism and *laissez-faire* capitalism bemoans: 'How often misused words generate misleading thoughts.[132]

44

Harry Daugherty, *see* Warren Gamiel Harding

Daughters of the American Revolution, *see* Franklin D. Roosevelt

Jack Dempsey, *see* Ronald W. Reagan

Commodore Stephen Decatur (1779–1820) was the American naval hero who, as Lieutenant Decatur, recaptured the *USS Philadelphia* in February 1804 during the Barbary wars against North African pirates.

'Decatur's Toast', given at a banquet at Norfolk (Virginia) in April 1816 was not '*My country right or wrong*', nor even '*Our country right or wrong.*' It was 'Our country! In her intercourse with foreign nations, may she always be in the right; but our country, right or wrong.'[133] Many American presidents, notably James Monroe (1817–25), he of the Monroe doctrine, and Theodore Roosevelt (1901–9), he of the big stick, have acted according to the common abbreviation of the toast and ignored Decatur's fine-tuning.

9th Duke of Devonshire, *see* Stanley Baldwin

Thomas E. Dewey, *see* Alice Roosevelt Longworth

Charles Dickens (1812–70), novelist. In *Bleak House*, Dickens quotes the catechism, '*To do my duty in that state of life unto which it has pleased God to call me.*' That was the popular misquotation of, 'To do my duty in that state of life unto which it **shall please** God to call me.'[134] A statement that allows for optimism. God may improve your station in life. The vernacular downgrading of the sentence reveals an unexpected vein of pessimism in the Victorians.

Howard Dietz, *see* Samuel Goldwyn *and* George Bernard Shaw

Viscount Dilhorne, *see* Traditional

Benjamin Disraeli (Earl of Beaconsfield, 1804–81), Conservative prime minister, British statesman.

The great political feud between Disraeli and the Liberal leader William Ewart Gladstone (1809–98) was sharpened by the sybaritism of the former and the puritanism of the latter. In intellect the two were evenly matched, but Gladstone lacked Disraeli's wit – typical of which was, *'I do not object so much to Gladstone having the ace of trumps up his sleeve as I do to his claiming the Almighty put it there.'* But Disraeli was only improving upon the words of the Liberal MP, Henry Labouchere, whose biographer wrote: 'Mr Labouchere's jest about Mr Gladstone laying upon Providence the responsibility of always placing the ace of trumps up his sleeve was a good one. In one of his private letters I find the quip worded a little more pungently. "[Gladstone] cannot refrain from perpetually bringing an ace down his sleeve, even when he only has to play fair to win the trick".'[135]

Disraeli also said: *'I wish I were as sure of anything as Gladstone is about everything'*, but an earlier prime minister, Viscount Melbourne (1779–1848), said it of his Secretary for War, Thomas Babington Macaulay (1st Baron Macaulay, q.v.).[136] Bartlett (1937) claims this has also been ascribed to William Windham (1750–1810) but this is improbable as Windham died aged sixty when Macaulay was only ten.[137] It was not Disraeli who likened the smile of Sir Robert Peel, the Edward Heath of his day, to 'the silver plate on a coffin', but the Irish MP, Daniel O'Connell.[138] Disraeli did say of

Gladstone: 'He made his conscience not his guide but his accomplice.'[139]

When asked who made the well-known comment, *'The Church of England is the Tory Party at prayer'*, most people will hazard 'Disraeli?' The surprise is not that Disraeli failed to say it but that nobody seems to know who did. In spite of being so well known, the aphorism is not in any of the established dictionaries of quotations. However *Brewer's Politics* published in 1993 states that a Congregationalist minister, Agnes Maud Royden (1887–1967) begot the phrase in a 1917 speech. 'The Church should no longer be satisfied to represent only the Conservative Party at prayer.'[140] It is not clear whether the lady is referring to her own church, the Church of England or English churches generally. What's more, she is as likely to be quoting an old aphorism as begetting a new one. This must be credited to Anon.

When Disraeli lay dying in April 1881 it was suggested the widowed Queen Victoria might visit him. 'No, it is better not. She would only ask me to take a message to Albert' – sometimes proffered as his last words. An alternative is that, dying, he corrected the proofs of his last speech as: *'I will not go down to posterity talking bad grammar.'* That was said some weeks earlier. As he died he said something to the faithful Montagu Corry (Lord Rowton). The words were inaudible, but a great man has to have last words, especially a Victorian, so we have his 'last authentically recorded words, April 1881' given as: 'I had rather live but I am not afraid to die', which is unbelievably out of character for the old cynic.[141] *See also* Francis I *and* Mark Twain.

Norman Douglas, *see* Lord Byron

Lord and Lady Douglas-Home of The Hirsel, *see* Traditional

Sir Arthur Conan Doyle (Dr Watson's literary agent), *see* Sherlock Holmes

Sir Francis Drake (1540?–96), the first Englishman to circumnavigate the globe. Licensed pirate.

Drake was playing bowls at Plymouth in 1588 when the sails of the Spanish armada, intent on invading England, were sighted. Sir Francis, famously displaying English sang-froid, declared: *'There is time to win the game and to thrash the Spaniards too.'* Or might have done, were it not for the fact that the tide was out and the fleet locked in the harbour. Besides which, no bowler abandons a match he is winning. The earliest reference to the comment is in W. Oldys's *Life of Raleigh* of 1736.[142]

Theodore Dreiser (1871–1945), the American novelist, is deservedly remembered for his lack of false modesty, or indeed of modesty of any sort. He carefully prepared his dying words, *'Shakespeare, I come'*,[143] but on his deathbed forgot to say them.

Not every critic shared Dreiser's view of Dreiser. 'His style is atrocious, his sentences are chaotic, his grammar and syntax faulty; he has no feeling for words, no sense of diction. His wordiness and his repetition are unbearable, his caco-phonies incredible', wrote T. K. Whipple.[144] Even so, Dreis-er's *An American Tragedy* (1925), was one of the best-selling books of interwar America.

John Dryden (1631–1700), poet, playwright and first official Poet Laureate. The unqualified dictum, *'Second*

thoughts are best,[145] was whittled down from Dyrden's highly qualified remark, almost a question, 'Second thoughts, **they say**, are best.' In the same era, Matthew Henry (1662–1714) wrote of '. . . second and sober thoughts', which perhaps provides an answer for Dryden. Either the Comte de Montrond or Talleyrand wrote: 'Have no truck with first impulses, they are always generous ones' (*'Defiez-vous des premiers mouvements parce qu'ils sont bons.'*)[146] Decide for yourself – then think again. *See also* William Shakespeare.

Major William Drury, *see* Samuel Pepys

Robert Dundas (1st Viscount Melville), *see* Richard Brinsley Sheridan

Isadora Duncan (1878–1927), the freestyle dancer with the tabloid 'private' life, was strangled when her long scarf caught in the wheel of her speeding open car. Nevertheless she had time to say 'Adieu my friends. I go on to glory',[147] and one of those friends was able to hear the words and write them down . . . and if you believe that you'll believe anything.

William Claude Dunkinfield, *see* W. C. Fields

Bishop of Durham, *see* Rt. Revd David Jenkins

Leo Durocher (1906–1991), one-time manager of the Brooklyn Dodgers baseball team.

Durocher encapsulated the American obsession with winning in 'Nice guys finish last', or thought he did. Before a game against the New York Giants on 6 July 1946 he said: 'Take a look at them. All nice guys. They'll finish last. Nice guys. Finish last.' The last two sentences were picked up, repeated and run together as *'Nice guys finish last.'*[148] Knute Rockne (q.v.) took the same approach. 'Rockne wanted nothing but "bad losers". Good losers get into the habit of losing.'[149] It was 'Red' Sanders, not Vince Lombardi, who added: 'Sure, winning isn't everything. It's the only thing.'[150] That approach to sport is not purely American. 'Some people think football is a matter of life and death. I don't take that attitude. I can assure you it is much more serious than that', said the British manager Bill Shankly.[151]

Yosef Vissarionovich Dzhugashvili, *see* Josef Stalin

E

Sir (Robert) Anthony Eden, 1st Earl of Avon, *see* R. A. Butler

Dwight D. Eisenhower, *see* General Douglas MacArthur

Ralph Waldo Emerson (1803–82) American essayist, philosopher and poet.

Many a dilettante has taken refuge in Emerson's *bon mot*, *'Consistency is the hobgoblin of little minds'*, whereas the actual passage from *Self-Reliance* is both more precise and ironic: 'A foolish consistency is the hobgoblin of little minds, adored by little statesmen and philosophers and divines. With consistency a great soul has simply nothing to do.'[152]

Though Emerson was a founder of transcendentalism, he is now best remembered as the patron saint of Yankee self-sufficiency and can-do. '*Build a better mousetrap, and the world will beat a path to your door*', has kept patent offices busy for over a hundred years, but is only attributed to Emerson and does not appear in this particular form in any of his writings. Mrs Sarah S. B. Yule copied the following extract into her notebook during an Emerson lecture and included it in her *Borrowings* (1889): '*If a man write a better book, preach a better sermon, or make a better mousetrap than his neighbour, tho' he build his house in the woods, the world will beat a path to his door.*'[153] Mrs Yule got it wrong too. What he said was: 'If a man has good corn, or wood, or boards, or pigs to sell, or can make better chairs, or knives, crucibles or church organs, than anybody else, you will find a broad, hard-beaten road to his house, though it be in the woods.'[154]

Needless to say, mousetrap technology has remained remarkably little changed over the last hundred years.

Zhou Enlai, *see* General Karl von Clausewitz

Desiderius Erasmus, *see* John Bright

Euripides Andromache, *see* Sir Walter Scott Bt.

F

Clifton Fadiman, *see* Samuel Goldwyn *and* Gertrude Stein

W. C. Fields (William Claude Dunkinfield, 1879–1946), American comedian and actor.

As Fields said 'Last week I went to Philadelphia – but

it was closed', he was the obvious man to have attributed to him as his last words: *'On the whole I'd rather be in Philadelphia.'* These were not Fields's invention, but appeared in the June 1925 issue of *Vanity Fair* as a joke epitaph. 'Here lies W. C. Fields. "On the whole I'd rather be in Philadelphia".'[155]

Another famous Fields line was: *'Anyone who hates animals and kids can't be all bad.'* But the actual quote wasn't by Fields but about him. It was used by the writer Leo Rosten when introducing Fields at the Masquers Club dinner on 16 February 1939, and the original words were: 'The only thing I can say about W. C. Fields, whom I have admired since the day he advanced upon Baby LeRoy with an ice pick, is this: any man who hates dogs and babies can't be all bad.'[156] Fields is alleged to have spiked Baby LeRoy's milk with gin and, when the child star couldn't perform, went around saying 'The kid's no trouper.'[157] *See also* Miss Mae West.

Jim Fisk, *see* Francis I

Grace Hodgson Flandrau, *see* Alice Roosevelt Longworth

Revd Lieutenant Howell Forgey, *see* Revd Captain William A. Maguire

Michael Foot, *see* The Oxford Union

Gerald Rudolph Ford, *see* Lyndon B. Johnson

Henry Ford (1863–1947) pioneer billionaire and eponymous automobile manufacturer. Ford became cranky in old age but not early enough to say *'History is bunk'* when only fifty-three. He told the *Chicago Tribune* reporter Charles N. Wheeler: 'History is **more or less** bunk. It's tradition. We don't want tradition. We want to live in the present and the only history that is worth a tinker's damn is the history we make today.'[158]

Ford was also the pioneer of assembly-line mass production which meant uniform products, fifteen million near-identical Model T. Fords to start with. Hence his famous statement, '*Any colour you like, so long as it's black.*' This was not his, but coined as an advertising slogan to hold the fort until, in 1925, Ford reluctantly gave in to public demand and started producing his cars in other colours.[159]

John Dillinger, the bank robber, once wrote Ford an unsolicited testimonial on the merits of the Ford as a getaway car. This was not used in the company's advertising.

Anatole France (Jacques-Anatole-François Thibault, 1844–1924), French man of letters and Nobel Prize laureate.

'*The law, in its majestic equality, forbids the rich as well as the poor to sleep under bridges, to beg in the street and to steal bread*', is much more aphoristic in English than the original French: '*La majestueuse égalité des lois, qui interdit au riche comme au pauvre de coucher sous les ponts, de mendier dans les rues et de voler du pain*', but less pithy than the earlier axiom from Lord Justice Matthew (Sir James Matthew, 1830–1908). 'In England, justice is open to all – like the Ritz Hotel.'[160] Variations on this, '"The law is equally open to the poor and rich. So is the London Tavern",' go back to the eighteenth century at least.[161]

Francis I (1494–1547), King of France, (1515–47). After suffering a number of military defeats, Francis I was captured in 1525 and imprisoned by Charles V in Madrid.

He wrote that 'Of all things there remains to me only honour and life which is safe.' ('*De toutes choses ne me'est demeure que l'honneur et la vie qui est sauve.*'[162]) Posthumous tidying-up has reduced this to '*All is lost save honour*.'[163] American 'entrepreneur' Jim Fisk made a liberal use of the axiom after an unsuccessful skirmish with J. Pierpont Morgan: 'Nothing is lost save honour!' While Richard Nixon (or was it Henry Kissinger?) characterized the ignominious American withdrawal from Vietnam in 1975 as 'Peace with honour.' Neville Chamberlain, British prime minister (1937–40) spoke to the press on arriving at Heston aerodrome, after his agreement with Hitler on 30 September 1938: 'I believe it is peace in our time . . . peace with honour.'[164] Chamberlain, no great phrasemaker, pinched it from Disraeli who, arriving at Downing Street from Berlin, said: 'Lord Salisbury and myself have brought you back peace – but a peace I hope with honour.'[165] Disraeli, a deft plagiarist himself, surely pinched it from somebody, probably Polybius (*c.* 208–126 BC) 'For peace with justice and honour is the fairest and most profitable of possessions.'[166]

Dizzy broke the most important rule for plagiarists, 'Thou shalt not get found out.' His funeral oration for the great Duke of Wellington was largely lifted from an article by Louis Thiers (pronounced 'Tears') on Marshal Laurent de Gouvion Saint-Cyr (pronounced '*sincere*'). Leigh Hunt's *Examiner* delivered a punishing rebuke:

> In sounding great Wellington's praise,
> > Dizzy's grief and his truth both appear
> For a flood of great Thiers he lets fall
> > Which were certainly meant for St-Cyr.[167]

Generalissimo Franciso Franco ('El Caudillo',

1892–1975), Fascist dictator of Spain from the end of the Spanish Civil War in 1939 to his death.

When Franco's forces, four columns strong, were besieging Madrid in 1936 during the Civil War, his protagonists inside the city were described as his *'fifth column'*. Following precedent, this was attributed to Franco rather than to his subordinate, General Emilio Mola, who actually coined the description.[168]

Frederick the Great, *see* Colonel William Preston

Christopher Fry, *see* Margaret Thatcher

G

Emile Gaboriau, *see* John Milton

Galileo Galilei (1564–1642), pioneer astronomer, is best remembered for *'Eppur si muove'* – 'And yet it moves', muttered *sotto voce* in 1633 when the Holy Office (the Inquisition) forced him to deny his belief that the earth revolved around the sun.

There is no record of these words being uttered by Galileo. A century after his death they were given him by the French writer Abbé Augustin Irailh in *Querelles Littéraires* and the Italian Giuseppe Baretti (1719–89) in the *Italian Library* 1757.[169]

Paul Gallico, *see* Gertrude Stein

Greta Garbo (1905–90), legendary Swedish film actress who died a recluse. Kenneth Tynan said, 'What when drunk one sees in other women, one sees in Garbo sober.'[170]

In appearance Miss Garbo had all the serene beauty, warmth and approachability of an iceberg – although in her early Hollywood years she was as available to the press as any other star. Eventually she got hooked on her own legend, typified by her most famous remark, '*I want to be alone*'. (Add heavy Swedish accent if desired.) What she actually said was 'I want to be **let** alone.' In the emerging Hollywood tradition William A. Drake wrote the line into the script of her 1932 film *Grand Hotel*, so she did, finally, say it.[171] For other examples *see* Miss Mae West *and* Messrs Laurel and Hardy. *See also* Ramon Novarro.

Guiseppe Garibaldi, *see* Benito Mussolini

David Garrick, *see* William Shakespeare

General Charles de Gaulle (1890–1970), leader of the Free French in the Second World War and later president of France, whose symbol was the two-bar patriarchal Cross of Lorraine.

Only de Gaulle could have made the breathtaking comment, upon meeting President Roosevelt for the first time in 1943, '*I am Joan of Arc. I am Clemenceau*', which manages to achieve the ultimate in both arrogance and humility at the same time. Or to be exact: only de Gaulle could have that breathtaking comment attributed to him, and have it believed. In fact that parody was made up by the President, who took as great and instant a dislike to de Gaulle as de Gaulle did to him.[172] As the story circulated, de Gaulle's *alter egos* allegedly came to include almost every

French hero except, curiously, Bonaparte. In de Gaulle's last years his isolation at Colombey-les-Deux-Eglises was almost as great as Bonaparte's on St Helena. Roosevelt's parody must have got back to de Gaulle – such things always do – and it may have inspired the dictum he gave to his staff at Mont-Valérian on 18 June 1946: 'Foch, Clemenceau, de Gaulle – it is the same thing.'[173]

De Gaulle didn't endear himself to Winston Churchill either. The British war leader confided to friends: 'The heaviest cross I have to bear is the cross of Lorraine.'

In 1960 it would have been helpful to France's powerful Communist Party if de Gaulle had said *'The evolution towards Communism is inevitable'*, but as he failed to do so they credited him with saying it anyway.[174]

Sir Eric Geddes (1857–1937), politician and member of the British War Cabinet in 1918.

In talking about German reparations after the Great War, Sir Eric promised to *'squeeze Germany till the pips squeak'*. What Sir Eric said at a speech in Cambridge was: 'The Germans . . . are going to pay every penny. They are going to be squeezed as the lemon is squeezed – until the pips squeak. My only doubt is not whether we can squeeze hard enough, but whether there is enough juice.'[175] Both versions of this quotation are often wrongly attributed to his brother, Sir Auckland Geddes, later first Baron Geddes.[176]

Denis Healey (now Lord Healey), when Labour's shadow Chancellor of the Exchequer, promised the Labour Party Conference of 1973 *'to squeeze the rich till the pips squeak'*[177] – if you believe the press. Lord Healey begs you not to.

> I warned Conference 'There are going to be howls of
> anguish from the eighty thousand people who are

rich enough to pay over seventy-five per cent on the last slice of their income.' ... I never said ... I would 'Squeeze the rich until the pips squeak', though I did quote Tony Crossland using this phrase of Lloyd George's [*sic*] in reference to property speculators, not the rich in general.[178]

In office, Chancellor Healey kept his promise to impose even higher taxes on the rich, but all this achieved was to divert the energies of entrepreneurs, managers and *rentiers* from creating new wealth to preserving what they had. Among the many morals to be drawn from Mr Healey's tale is to remember that all political party conferences have a collective IQ of about half the sum of their parts, and the political press corps about twice. *See also* James Callaghan.

George V (1865–1936), King and Emperor, 1910–36. A man's dying words can be as fiercely fought over as his estate. (*See*, for example, Charles Darwin *and* William Pitt, the Younger.) When the man is a king, those words have a social and political significance – or used to.

When George V died, *The Times* reported his dying words as: '*How is the Empire?*'[179] commonly rendered as: '*Is all well with the Empire?*' The irreverent claimed that 'Queen Mary said to him "When you're better, dear, you can go to Bognor to recuperate", at which His Majesty, who had been a serving naval officer, replied characteristically: "*Bugger Bognor*", and expired.' In 1986 it was revealed that Lord Dawson of Penn, the King's doctor, had kept His Majesty sedated for his last hours and so arranged matters that his death occurred in time for the 'responsible' morning papers to report it, rather than the more 'sensational' evening papers. As Lord Moynihan, a medical colleague of Dawson's, put it:

> Lord Dawson of Penn
> Has killed lots of men.
> So that's why we sing
> God save the King

So George V had no dying words. His last words were almost certainly those to his final Council of State held in his bedroom at Sandringham. 'Gentlemen, I am sorry for keeping you waiting like this, I am unable to concentrate.'[180] *See also* William Pitt, the Younger *and* Sir James Melville.

David Lloyd George (1st Earl Lloyd George of Dwyfor, 1863–1945), politician, 1890–1945, statesman, 1916–18, prime minister, 1916–22. 'He was the first prime minister since Walpole to leave office flagrantly richer than he entered it, the first since the Duke of Grafton to live openly with his mistress.'[181]

On Armistice Day, 11 November 1918, Lloyd George told the House of Commons: 'At eleven o'clock this morning came to an end the cruellest and most terrible war that has ever scourged mankind. I hope we may say that thus, this fateful morning, came to an end all wars',[182] not *'the war to end wars'* usually attributed to him. Americans usually credit the phrase to President Woodrow Wilson (q.v.) who used it in 1919. Originally it came from the title of a book by H. G. Wells, *The War That Will End War* published in 1914.[183] Wells later remarked, 'I launched the phrase "the war to end war", and that was not the least of my crimes.'[184]

As the troops returned home to demobilization they were cheered by the prime minister's promise to create *'a land fit for heroes to live in'*. Lloyd George made no such promise. 'What is our task? To make Britain a fit country for heroes to live in'[185] is what he, oh so carefully, said.

'What do you think happens to Mr Lloyd George when he is alone in the room?', Lady Violet Bonham-Carter asked John Maynard Keynes. 'When he is alone in the room there is nobody there', replied the economist, whose intelligence won even Bertrand Russell's respect.[186] *See also* Lord Hugh Cecil.

Edward Gibbon (1737–94), the historian, is claimed by both the cynics and the pessimists as one of their own.

Gibbon wrote of *The Decline and Fall of the Roman Empire*: 'My English text is chaste, and all the licentious passages are left in the obscurity of a learned language', usually misquoted as: '*the decent obscurity of a dead language*'. Or, as sardonic classics masters used to tell their pupils, 'If you want to read the dirty bits you'll have to learn Latin.'

Gibbon's aphorism on religion was oft repeated. '*All religions seem to the people equally true, to the philosopher equally false and to the magistrate equally useful.*' Gibbon's text in chapter II of *The Decline and Fall* began: 'The various modes of worship which prevailed in the Roman world were all considered by the peoples as equally true . . .' *et cetera*. Gibbon was reporting the opinions of others, not voicing his own.

It was the Duke of Gloucester (1743–1805) who said to Gibbon, upon being presented with the second volume of *The Decline and Fall*, 'Another damned thick, square book! Always scribble, scribble, scribble! Eh! Mr Gibbon?' and not the Duke of Cumberland, nor King George III, two of his brothers.[187] *See also* Napoleon Bonaparte.

George Gipp, *see* Knute Rockne

William Ewart Gladstone, *see* Benjamin Disraeli

George Glass, *see* Marlon Brando

Hannah Glasse, *see* Mrs Beeton

Hermann Goering (1893–1946). As the only Nazi leader with a passion for music, pictures, sculpture and architecture (especially other people's), Goering was the inevitable choice to be credited with *'Wenn ich Kulture hore ... entsichere ich meinen Browning!'* Popularly, *'When I hear the word "culture" ... I reach for my gun'*, but correctly: 'Whenever I hear the word "culture" ... I release the safety-catch of my Browning!'[188]

That assertion was coined by the playwright Hanns Johst, but he didn't say it either. He put it into the mouth of a character in his play *Schlageter*, first produced in Berlin in 1934.[189] Johst was lucky: many writers have created evil characters, written dialogue for them and then found those words quoted as their own views.

The Golden Rule is, I think, as old as philosophy but no older. The Rule was first recorded as by Confucius in around 500 BC: 'What you do not want others to do to you, do not do to others',[190] and has been echoed by every succeeding generation. Jesus put it simply (much better than either St Matthew or St Luke[191]) 'Love thy neighbour as thyself' (when he was quoting the Old Testament).[192] The old English toast is the most involved version: 'When we and ours have it in our power to do for you and yours what you and yours have done for us and ours, then we and ours will do for you and yours what you and yours have done for us and ours'[193] – but the purpose of that toast is not to impart wisdom but to enjoy the inebriated proposer's attempts to say it correctly.

There are numerous versions of the Golden Rule, and none of them the definitive one.

Samuel Goldwyn (1882–1974), film producer and Hollywood tsar, immigrated to the United States from Poland at thirteen.

Goldwyn became and remains famous for his mangling of the English language – 'If people won't go to the cinema there's nothing you can do to stop them' – yet most Goldwynisms are as spurious as most Spoonerisms (q.v.). Irving Fein said of his time as assistant publicity director to Goldwyn: 'We used to make up Goldwynisms all the time in order to get publicity breaks.'[194] He and many others, including stand-up comics such as Eddie Cantor.

'*I can answer you in two words, "im-possible"*'.[195] This is quoted as a Goldwynism, citing the very source, which continues: '. . . but Sam did not say it.* It was printed late in 1925 in a humorous magazine and credited to an anonymous Potash or Perimutter.'[196] Charlie Chaplin claimed to have invented that quip.[197]

When Goldwyn tried to persuade Orson Welles to make a film for him he did not say, '*Look Orson, if you'll just say yes to doing a picture with me I'll give you a blanket check right now*', but 'a blank check'. The twist was thought up by an eavesdropping reporter. When the *Reader's Digest* sent Goldwyn an unsolicited cheque for twenty-five dollars for quoting it in the 'Picturesque Patter of Speech' column, he was not amused. The following Goldwynisms are also counterfeit.

'*Our comedies are not to be laughed at*', is as old as Hollywood slapstick. '*Never let that sonofabitch into this office again – until we need him*' is also a traditional Hollywood witticism and has

* Most dictionaries of quotations are unreliable – except this one.

been attributed to Louis B. Mayer, Harry Cohn, et al., as well as to Goldwyn.

'*It rolls off my back like a duck.*' George Oppenheimer, one-time Hollywood scriptwriter, claimed the credit. 'I remember springing it for the first time on Dotty Parker and Edna Ferber when we were all sitting round the writers' table in the commissary one day', and he won the prize for the best Goldwynism the lunchers could think up, each having contributed ten dollars to the pot.

'*Quick as a flashlight*' was one of Irving Fein's.[198]

'*When I see the pictures you play at that theatre it makes the hair stand on the edge of my seat.*' Not Goldwyn, but the Hungarian-born Michael Curtiz talking to Louis B. Mayer.[199] When directing *The Charge of the Light Brigade* in 1936, he delighted David Niven by calling: 'Bring on the empty horses.'[200] '*The next time I send a damn fool for something, I go myself*' was also Curtiz,[201] who won the 1943 Best Director Oscar for *Casablanca*.

When Lillian Hellman's play *The Children's Hour* was a Broadway hit Goldwyn discussed buying the screen rights. He was told: 'Forget it. It's about lesbians', but he did not reply: '*Don't worry about that. We'll make them Americans.*' The suggestion that Goldwyn – a kingpin in the anything-goes-so-long-as-you-don't-shock-the-public Hollywood – did not know what lesbians were, is risible. Besides, Hellman was under contract to him as a scriptwriter, they met regularly and Goldwyn produced *The Children's Hour* as *These Three* in 1936. The twist in the tale is that, due to the strict 'family values' of the Hays Office, Goldwyn actually did 'make them Americans'. Lesbianism was excised from the script.

When told a script was too caustic: '*To hell with the cost. If it's a good story I'll make it.*'[202] Phoney.

'*I read part of it all the way through.*' Fake.

'*We can get all the Indians we need at the reservoir.*'
Counterfeit.

When he was ill: '*I was on the brink of the abscess.*'
Bogus.

'*Anyone who would go to a psychiatrist ought to have his head examined.*' This sensible witticism, also attributed to Lillian Hellman, is as old as psychiatry.

Any allegedly written Goldwynisms are also certain to be spurious. Highly paid secretaries made sure of that. Thus, after Goldwyn made a film of Thurber's *Walter Mitty*, he did not cable the author: '*I'm very sorry you thought I was too blood and thirsty.*' *Ergo*, Thurber did not reply: '*Not only did I think so but I was horror and struck.*'

'*A verbal contract isn't worth the paper it's written on*' is almost a genuine Goldwynism. He once said of Joseph M. Schenck – whose probity was a rarity in Hollywood – 'His verbal contract is worth more than the paper it's printed on.'[203]

In later years Goldwyn denied ever saying '*Gentlemen, include me out*', at a meeting of the Motion Picture Producers and Distributors of America in October 1933. However it is probably genuine, despite Goldwyn's ambiguous remarks at Balliol, Oxford, on 1 March 1945: 'For years I have been known for saying "include me out", but today I am giving it up for ever.'[204]

The more one looks into Sam Goldwyn's alleged malapropisms, the more difficult it is to find reliable evidence for any of them. As he said: 'Goldwynisms! Don't talk to me about Goldwynisms. You want to hear some Goldwynisms, go talk to Jesse Lasky.'[205]

Two typical, and genuine, Goldwynisms are : 'Pictures are for entertainment. Messages should be sent by Weston Union',[206] and: 'Why should people go out and pay to see

64

bad movies when they can stay at home and see bad television for nothing?'[207] But those are simply witty.

Goldwyn was reported as saying, as he looked at the huge crowds at Louis B. Mayer's funeral: '*As I always say, give the people what they want and they'll turn out to see it.*' However Goldwyn did not attend Mayer's funeral and, anyway, the story is told about the funerals of most of the Hollywood tsars, usually with one of the survivors speaking the punchline. For example, *Oxford Modern Quotations* attributes the epigram to 'Red' Skelton at Harry Cohn's funeral in 1958.

Goldwyn's dying words were, inevitably, a Goldwynism: '*I never thought I'd live to see the day*' and, inevitably, counterfeit. Clifton Fadiman dreamed them up.[208] *See also* George Bernard Shaw.

Barnabe Googe, *see* William Shakespeare

Lady Gough, *see* Anon.

D. M. Graham, *see* The Oxford Union

James Edward Grant, *see* John Wayne

Thomas Gray, *see* William Shakespeare

Horace Greeley (1811–72), American journalist. Even the magisterial 1942 *Oxford Dictionary of Quotations* credits Greeley with the advice '*Go West, young man*', although the 1985 edition also credits this advice to John Soule in the *Terre Haut Express* in 1851.[209] In fact these words belong solely to Soule. When Greeley quoted them in the *New York Tribune* he gave Soule full attribution.[210] In England 'to go West' used to mean to be hanged at Tyburn (now Marble Arch) to the West of London.

Graham Greene (1904–91), traveller, author, scriptwriter.

In Carol Reed's 1949 film, *The Third Man*, Orson Welles (playing Harry Lime) says: '*In Italy for thirty years under the Borgias they had warfare, terror, murder and bloodshed* – they produced Michelangelo, Leonardo da Vinci and the Renaissance. In Switzerland they had brotherly love, five hundreds years of democracy and peace and what did that produce . . .? The cuckoo clock*', and pedants and pundits have pointed out that these were not Welles's words but those of Graham Greene, who wrote the filmscript. In fact the words really are Welles's, interpolated by him into Greene's script.[211]

Sir Thomas Gresham (1519–79), founded the Royal Exchange, in the City of London, in 1568. He lived in an age when rulers had reacquired the habit of debasing their coinage – using less gold or silver and more base metals. Contemporary entrepreneurs added to the problem by 'clipping' a small amount of gold or silver from all the coins they could process. Gresham's Law states: '*Bad money drives out good but good money does not drive out bad.*'

The original is more exact: '*Where two coins are of equal legal value but unequal in intrinsic value, the one having the lesser intrinsic value tends to remain in circulation and the other to be hoarded or exported*', but that was not coined by Sir Thomas

---

* In spite of the fact that Pope Alexander VI (Rodrigo Borgia) introduced the censorship of books, the Borgias were no worse than other powerful families of the Italian Renaissance. The evidence of their evil ways was faked during the papacy of Julius II, who succeeded Alexander in 1503 (bar the 26-day Papacy of Pius III, who was probably poisoned by Julius).

either. He gained credit for this truism – which had already been set out by Nicholas Oresme and Nicholaus Copernicus – because he explained its working to Queen Elizabeth.

Gresham's Law has found wide application, for example in television. 'Any entertainment programme, no matter how bad, will drive out any public affairs programme, no matter how good.'[212]

Intellectual masochists can enjoy a real treat by studying Gresham's Law in conjunction with bimetallism – gold and silver coinage in concurrent circulation – and inflation.

H

Richard Haldane, 1st Viscount Haldane of Cloan (1856–1928), British lawyer, philosopher and statesman. Appointed Lord Chancellor in the Liberal government of 1912.

Haldane was hounded out of office in 1915 because the public believed he had said *'Germany is my spiritual home.'* An academic foe, one Professor Oncken, distorted Haldane's remark, made to Mrs Humphrey Ward the novelist: 'Yes. I consider Lotze's classroom to be my spiritual home.'[213] Haldane returned to office as Minister of Labour in the first Labour government of 1924.

General Kurt von Hammerstein, *see* General Karl von Clausewitz

Warren Gamiel Harding (1865–1923) is a strong candidate for the title of America's Worst President (1921–3) although nobody can have been quite as bad as the twenty-ninth president is now perceived.

At the Republicans' 1920 Chicago Convention the Ohio politician, Harry Daugherty, wrote:

> The convention will be deadlocked and, after the candidates have gone to their limit, some twelve or fifteen men, worn out and bleary-eyed from lack of sleep, will sit down about two o'clock in the morning in a smoke-filled room in some hotel and decide the nomination. When that time comes Harding will be selected.

And so it was. In Suite 404–6 of the Blackstone Hotel Harding was offered the Republican nomination, although the term 'smoke-filled room' had earlier been applied to the Caucus Club that ran Boston in the eighteenth century. Harding, an addicted poker player, famously explained his victory: '*We drew a pair of deuces and filled*' or, in lay terms, he claimed he played a poor hand well.

This sound, homely phrase appears in *Our Times*, a book by a journalist, Mark Sullivan, who was with Harding throughout his successful presidential campaign. The footnote is never quoted. Sullivan writes that Harding may have made the remark, 'Or he may never have said it – it may have been some reporter's conception of what he ought to say.'[214] Truth may be stranger than fiction but often lacks the staying power of a well-turned lie.

Harding, who may or may not have known just how corrupt his administration had become, was lucky to die in office.

Oliver Hardy (1892–1957), was two-thirds of the comedy

duo, Laurel and Hardy, the other third being the British-born Arthur Stanley Jefferson (1890–1965), known as Stan Laurel, who wrote most of their gags, one-liners and catch-phrases.

Ollie did not say to Stan '*Here's another fine mess you've gotten me into*', nor did Laurel write it for him. The actual phrase was: 'Here's another **nice** mess you've gotten me into.' However Hollywood always catches up with demotic variations of famous lines – see Mae West and Greta Garbo – and in 1930 the pair made a thirty-minute film titled *Another Fine Mess*. (This has Stan and Ollie, on the run from the cops, disguised as master and maid.)[215]

J. Milton Hayes, *see* Rudyard Kipling

Denis Healey (now Lord Healey), *see* Sir Eric Geddes

Edward Heath (1916–), British politican and one-term prime minister (1970–74).

Heath is remembered by the British public for his promise during the 1970 general election '*to cut prices at a stroke*' if he and his party won. It says much about the public that they believed this impossible promise and then damned Heath for failing to fulfil it. Heath – whose main problem is being so intelligent he can't understand ordinary people – never said anything so silly. He did not talk of cutting prices nor even of stopping prices rising; he talked only of reducing the rate at which prices rose. 'The alternative is to break into the wages/prices spiral by acting directly to reduce prices. This can be done by reducing those taxes which bear directly on prices and costs, such as the Selective Employment Tax, and by taking a firm grip on public sector prices and charges such as coal, steel, gas, electricity, transport and postal charges. This would, at a stroke, reduce the **rise** in prices, increase production and reduce unemployment.'[216]

Heath's only memorable phrase is his description of the international holding company, Lonrho Ltd, and its chief executive, 'Tiny' R. W. Rowland, as *'the unacceptable face of capitalism'*. He actually said: 'It is the unpleasant and unacceptable face of capitalism', and he wasn't talking about Lonrho and Rowland in general but about one specific matter; the payment of certain directors' fees into bank accounts in a tax haven, the Cayman Islands.[217] It was typical of Heath that in 1973, with top tax rates then at seventy-five per cent, his puritan soul was amazed and appalled when people took legitimate measures to minimize their tax bills. Heath was acutely embarrassed as Lord Duncan-Sandys, one of the directors who had made use of the Caymans ploy, was a former Cabinet colleague of his. But then Heath was easily embarrassed. What added a surreal air to the whole imbroglio was the rumour that the original text for Heath's speech referred to 'this unacceptable **facet** of capitalism', but that a secretary ignorant of the word 'facet' changed it to 'face'.

Joseph Heller (1923–), American author. In his satire, *Catch-22* (1961), Joseph Heller wilfully and mischievously misquotes Shakespeare's *Twelfth Night*: *'Some men are born mediocre, some men achieve mediocrity, and some men have mediocrity thrust upon them. With Major Major it had been all three.'*[218]

Lillian Hellmann, *see* Samuel Goldwyn

William Ernest Henley, *see* Coventry Patmore

Val Hennessy of the *Daily Mail*, like all book reviewers, has suffered at the pens of publishers' publicists. Most of us will stretch the truth a little, some of us will stretch it to a Munchausian degree, but the publisher's publicist has a vocation that is above mere truth.

Ms Hennessy wrote of Martin Amis's *Einstein's Monsters*: 'In five cataclysmic short stories Amis crafts perplexing visions of the post-nuclear holocaust world, highlighting schizophrenia, rape, brutality and suppurating despair . . . Frankly I couldn't understand what Amis was banging on about most of the time, it is eighty per cent unreadable.' Then the paperback edition of *Einstein's Monsters* appeared with the triumphal quote '. . . *perplexing visions of the post-nuclear holocaust world*'. Pan shares Penguin's specialized sense of honesty. Ms Hennessy wrote of Richard Compton Miller's *Who's Really Who*: 'Only totally moronic people will rush out and buy this book', but Pan précised this into '*people will rush out and buy this book.*' The Grafton paperback of Anita Brookner's *Fraud* carried the encomium from Caroline Moore of *The Times* 'Classic Brookner' without mentioning that, in Ms Moore's view, 'classic Brookner' actually means 'A fictional atmosphere [that] is claustrophobic, heavy with muted frustration and muffled desires: airless feminine emotions without object or outlet, where the strongest feelings – self-pity, despair, resentment – are kept decently shrouded in dust-sheets.'[219]

Henri IV, King of France (1553–1610). In the fashion of the time all the best quotes were attributed to the King, but it was probably his chief minister, the great duc de Sully, who said in 1593 when the King converted to Catholicism for purely political reasons: '*Paris vaut bien une messe*', or 'Paris is well worth a Mass.' Henri's description of King James I of England (and VI of Scotland) as '*the wisest fool in Christendom*' is also probably Sully's, not the King's.[220] For another example *see* General John Pershing. *See also* Herbert Hoover.

Matthew Henry, *see* John Dryden

Patrick Henry (1736–99). The Demosthenes of the War of Independence; the great orator who roused colonial America to throw off the shackles of British rule. Or not.

Generations of Americans have been inspired by Henry's eloquent declamation in the Virginia Assembly on 20 March 1775: '*I know not what course others may take; but as for me, give me liberty or give me death*', ever since it was invented in 1818 by his biographer, William Wirt, who had never met, seen or heard him.[221]

Nor is there any evidence that Henry said '*Caesar had his Brutus, Charles the First his Cromwell and George the Third* ['Treason' cried the Speaker] *may profit by their example. If this be treason, make the most of it*', to the Virginia House of Burgesses in May 1765. Nobody at the time made any note of such sonorous wit. Another of Mr Wirt's nifties. Nor is: '*I am not a Virginian, but an American*' other than risible. Henry was the anti-Federalist who looked upon the alliance of the States as a temporary measure, needed only while fighting for independence.

Jefferson said of Henry: 'When he had spoken in opposition to my opinion, had produced a great effect – and I myself had been highly delighted and moved – I have asked myself when it ceased "What the devil has he said?" and could never answer the inquiry.'[222]

Katherine Hepburn, *see*, of course, Spencer Tracy

Heraclitus, *see* John Milton

John Heywood, *see* the Bible *and* William Shakespeare

Claude Helvetius, *see* Voltaire

Lord and Lady Hillingdon, *see* Anon.

Adolf Hitler (1889–1945), the paradigm of charismatic evil. Hitler's demands for '*Lebensraum*' – 'living space' for the German people, prompted the belief that he coined the word. He didn't. He expropriated it from Professor Karl Haushofer who developed the idea from the Swedish geographer Rudolph Kjellen's concept of 'geopolitics' which was, in turn, developed from the ideas of a German, Friedrich Ratzel, who concluded that a state, like all other living entities, must either grow or die.[223]

Edward W. Hoch (1849–1945), owner of the *Marion Record* of Kansas. Mr Hoch is usually credited with the maudlin lines that appeared in his paper:

> There is so much good in the worst of us
> And so much bad in the best of us
> That it hardly behoves any of us
> To talk about the rest of us.

. . . but Mr Hoch denied authorship of these twee sentiments which, by default, must now be ascribed to Anon. (q.v.).[224]

Sherlock Holmes (1887–1927). The best-known words of Sir Arthur Conan Doyle's great detective are: '*Elementary, my dear Watson*', but these do not appear in any of the fifty-six short stories and four novels about Holmes and Dr John Watson.

They were used by the South African actor, Basil

Rathbone (for many the definitive Holmes), who first used them in one of a sequence of pre-war Holmes and Watson films. In *The Return of Sherlock Holmes* (1929) Watson says: 'Amazing, Holmes', and the Great Detective replies: 'Elementary, my dear Watson, elementary.'[225] The closest the canon gets is in *The Crooked Man*, where Dr Watson writes: '"Excellent" I cried. "Elementary" said he.'

Herbert Hoover (1874–1964) was one of America's scapegoat presidents (1929–33) blamed for the Great Depression. Even the name of the massive Hoover Dam in Colorado, the highest in America at 221 metres/721 feet, was changed to the Boulder Dam until President Truman restored the original name in 1947. Hoover was a self-made millionaire and a true philanthropist.

He lives in folklore as the man who called Prohibition (1919–33) *'a noble experiment'*, but that expression was wished on him by his opponents. Hoover never said anything so fatuous, his actual words being: 'Our country has deliberately undertaken a great social and economic experiment, noble in motive and far-reaching in purpose.'[226] Nor did he say 'Prosperity is just around the corner.'

Hoover is usually credited with a Republican campaign slogan of 1932 promising to put *'a chicken in every pot'*. The American voter found this appeal to his peasant instincts patronizing – but the slogan wasn't Hoover's and wasn't original. Henri IV of France (q.v.) said at his coronation in 1589: 'I hope to make France so prosperous that every peasant will have a chicken in his pot each Sunday.' (*'Je veux qu'il n'y ait si pauvre en mon royaume qu'il n'ait tous les dimanches sa poule au pot.'*[227]) In 1610 Henri died of what counted as natural causes for a king in those days: assassination. French chicken consumption was still below target.

Herbert Hoover was unrelated to W. F. Hoover, eponym of the vacuum cleaner which was actually invented by J. Murray Spangler. Nor was he related to the unlamented head of the FBI, J. Edgar Hoover, of whom President Lyndon Johnson (q.v.) said: 'It's probably better to have him inside the tent pissing out than outside pissing in.'[228] *See also* Will Rogers.

J. Edgar Hoover, *see* Herbert Hoover

A. E. Housman, *see* Bertrand Russell

Sir Geoffrey Howe (Lord Howe of Abaravon), *see* R. A. Butler

Elbert Hubbard, *see* Frank Ward O'Malley

Sir David Hunt, *see* Harold Macmillan

James Henry Leigh Hunt, *see* Francis I

Aldous Huxley, *see* Alexander Pope

I

Harold Ickes, *see* Ronald W. Reagan

Robert G. Ingersoll (1833–99). Two groups are more practised than all others in misquoting their opponents and inventing quotations to ascribe to them: Christian churchmen and democratic politicians. As Boller and George delicately write: 'Even so stout a defender of McCarthy as William F. Buckley Jr. acknowledged that the Wisconsin senator had a habit of putting into direct quotes what amounted to a paraphrase of what he thought their position was.'[229] Senator McCarthy and many others.

Mr Ingersoll, as the professional agnostic who said: 'An honest God is the noblest work of man,' fell foul of the churchmen. Billy Sunday, the born-again believer in Jesus Christ whose followers are enjoined to 'Rejoice in the truth', quoted Ingersoll in a sermon on 26 May 1912. *'I would rather be the humblest peasant that ever lived . . . at peace with the world than be the greatest Christian that ever lived.'* Ingersoll was then safely dead and so in no position to call Mr Sunday an unchristian liar. The quotation was a corruption of words Ingersoll uttered at the tomb of Napoleon Bonaparte: 'I . . . would rather have been a French peasant and worn wooden shoes . . . than to have been that imperial impersonation of force and murder known as Napoleon the Great.'[230] (In England Mr Ingersoll's comment on an honest God is, of course, Mr Samuel Butler's comment on an honest God, but Mr Butler was only quoting Alexander Pope.[231])

A journalist – interviewing Ingersoll in his extensive library of books on atheism, agnosticism and related subjects – asked the owner what the collection cost and received the reply: 'These books cost me the governorship of Illinois and maybe the presidency of the United States.'[232]

Alanus de Insulis, *see* William Shakespeare

J

Andrew Jackson (1767–1845), American soldier and seventh American president (1829–37) did not say *'To the victor ... the spoils.'* New York Senator William L. Marcy (1786–1857) did. Speaking in the Senate Chamber in 1832 he was defending Martin van Buren, whose sophisticated use of political patronage when Governor of New York had been attacked by Henry Clay. 'It may be, sir, that the politicians of the United States are not so fastidious as some gentlemen are, as to disclosing the principles on which they act. They boldly practise what they preach. When they are contending for victory, they avow their intention of enjoying the fruits of it. If they are defeated, they expect to retire from office. They see nothing wrong in the rule that to the victors belong the spoils of the enemy.'[233] The personal exploitation of the public office has become less brazen since then. Naturally the idea is as old as conflict, civil or military. The earliest surviving expression of it is from Aurelius Propertius (b. *circa* 51 BC) in 22 BC. Anon. added pithily: 'The trouble is, there are always more victors than spoils.'

James I of England and VI of Scotland, *see* Henri IV

Henry James, *see* Winston L. S. Churchill, the *News of the World and* Anthony Trollope

Thomas Jefferson (1743–1826), third president of the United States, 1801–9. Jefferson is credited with writing the magnificent words of the American Declaration of Independence, including the moving sentence:

> We hold these truths to be self-evident, that all men
> are created equal, that they are endowed by their
> Creator with certain inalienable Rights, that among
> these are Life, Liberty and the pursuit of happiness.

Jefferson was a Virginian and that sentence is a neat abbreviation of a line from the Virginia Declaration of Rights which, in turn, took the phrase 'the pursuit of happiness' from the philosopher, John Locke. Jefferson's draft of the Declaration of Independence was first extensively edited by the Committee of Five. Then Congress made forty changes to the text, deleting 630 words and adding 146.[234] This is a rare instance, possibly unique, of two committees editing a government document and it emerging the better for it.

By the standards of his time Jefferson was a liberal and enlightened man, but is now damned by the politically correct as a slave-owner. Among his best-known aphorisms, not to be found in his works and speeches, is *Eternal vigilance is the price of liberty.* The probable parent of this truism is John Curran (1750–1817), speaking on 10 July 1790 on the right of election of the Lord Mayor of Dublin, when he said: 'The condition upon which God hath given liberty to man is eternal vigilance', and then he continues: 'which condition if he break, servitude is at once the consequence of his crime, and the punishment of his guilt.' Cynics will feel no surprise on being reminded that his sentiment has been used by self-proclaimed patriots, such as Senator Joseph McCarthy, to curtail liberty.

Equally well known is: *He governs best who governs least,*

but it is not Jefferson's nor even Ronald Reagan's. Henry David Thoreau, the American naturalist, who used it in his famous essay *Civil Disobedience* in 1849, has been credited with the aphorism but he knew better, putting it between inverted commas to indicate he was quoting: '*That best government is that which governs not at all.*' The original is Thomas Paine's: 'That government is best which governs least.'[235] *See also* Patrick Henry *and* George Washington.

Jesus Christ, *see* the Bible, Robert G. Ingersoll *and* Julian the Apostate

The Rt. Revd David Jenkins (1925–), was consecrated Bishop of Durham in York Minster in 1984. Shortly afterwards he wrote a letter to the *Church Times* which convinced the great British public he had denied the virgin birth of Jesus Christ. Then lightning struck York Minster, causing severe damage. Many people saw this as an obvious sign of God's displeasure at Mr Jenkins's elevation. (Although none of them explained why God should damage a great church erected to His glory rather than having the lightning strike the new bishop.) Bishop Jenkins was a teacher of theology for most of his career, used to forcing his students to think. What he actually wrote was: 'I wouldn't put it past God to arrange a virgin birth if He wanted to, but I very much doubt if He would – because it seems to be contrary to the way in which He deals with persons and brings His wonders out of natural personal relationships'[236] – and any ordained who isn't set thinking by that would do better joining the most obtuse of fundamentalist sects.

Lyndon Baines Johnson (1908–73), the thirty-sixth

president of the United States of America (1963–9), was as foul-mouthed a man as ever occupied the White House.

Johnson's expletives were worthier of deletion than the comparatively mild profanities of President Richard Nixon. Johnson's comment on President Gerald Ford, as the press reported it, was: *'Gerry's the only man I know who can't walk and chew gum at the same time.'* In fact it was: 'Gerry's the only man I know who can't fart and chew gum at the same time.' This unforgettable slander probably cost Ford the White House, which he lost narrowly to Jimmy Carter in 1976.[237] *See also* Herbert Hoover.

Dr Samuel Johnson (1709–84). Sage, writer and pioneer lexicographer.

One of the best-known darts from Johnson's *A Dictionary of the English Language* (1755) is his definition of 'fishing' as *'A fool at one end of the line and a worm at the other.'* The sentiment is outside argument. To the angler it shows culpable stupidity and ignorance of a fine sport requiring subtlety, determination, patience and skill. To the non-fisherman it is an uninteresting factual statement, so obvious as to be banal. All of which is moot, as Johnson defined fishing as simply: 'Commodity of taking fish.'

Johnson did write *'Patriotism is the last refuge of a scoundrel'*,[238] but it was not intended to be parotted by the ignorant and illiterate to 'prove' that all self-proclaimed patriots are covert scoundrels and overt hypocrites. Rather, he was making the point that many scoundrels take refuge in the decent camouflage of patriotism. For a perfect example, *see* Horatio Bottomley.

Every brandy-lush (a very different species to, say, a vodka-lush) can quote Johnson inaccurately. *'Claret for boys; port for men; brandy for heroes'*, but even when they quote it correctly: 'Claret is the liquor for boys; port for men; but he who aspires to be a hero must drink brandy', they never conclude the quotation to put it in context:

> ... brandy will do soonest for a man what drinking can do for him. There are indeed few who are able to drink brandy. That is a power rather to be wished for than attained.[239]

See also Harold Macmillan, James Otis, William Pitt, the Elder *and* Richard Brinsley Sheridan.

(John) Paul Jones (b. John Paul, 1747–92), naval officer. There is a dichotomy between British and American sources when they come to Jones. To the British he is a renegade Scottish smuggler, slaver and mercenary who served in the American, French and Russian navies. In the United States he is one of the great American heroes of the War of Independence.[240]

On 23 September 1779 Jones, on the *Bonhomme Richard* and in command of a squadron of three French ships and one American, was fighting the *Serapis* and another British ship off Flamborough Head on the Yorkshire coast. The *Bonhomme Richard* began to sink and the British admiral courteously asked Jones if he had struck his flag. '*I have not yet begun to fight*', is Jones's famous reply. Yet there is no contemporary evidence that Jones gave that answer, if he gave any at all: it is absent from his own record of the battle and if he had made such a choice comment he would not have left it out of his report.[241] Jones's four ships went on to capture both British ships.

Jones died in Paris, thus anticipating the injunction of Thomas Gold Appleton (1812–84): 'Good Americans, when they die, go to Paris.' Wilde pinched the phrase and used it in *The Picture of Dorian Gray* (1891) and again in *A Woman of No Importance* (1893). Wilde was a habitual plagiarist. Hence James MacNeil Whistler's response when Wilde said of one of his witticisms *I wish I'd said that*; 'You will Oscar, you will.'

Ben Jonson (*c*. 1573–1637), playwright, is occasionally accused of writing the plays of Shakespeare, but more to annoy the Baconians than through any passionately held beliefs. (It was P. G. Wodehouse who concluded that the works of Shakespeare had not been written by William Shakespeare, but by another man of the same name.[242] *See also* Francis Bacon.)

Sir John Young paid a stonemason 18d (7.5 new pence) to carve the inscription on Jonson's memorial for Westminster Abbey, and it read: *'O rare Ben Jonson.'* It should have been 'Orare Ben Jonson', that is, 'Pray for Ben Jonson' but, it seems, the mason felt short-changed. Once the memorial was in place, however, it was easier to pretend the inscription was correct than to reject the stone.[243] *See also* Miss Mae West.

Julian, called 'The Apostate' (Flavius Claudianus Julius *c*. 332–63), the Emperor of Rome *c*. 361–3, who never set foot in Rome while Emperor.

We didn't need George Orwell to tell us that the victors write, or more usually rewrite, history. 'Who controls the past controls the future: who controls the present controls the past.'[244] The victors include those who outlive their enemies. Julian's enemies included the nascent Christian church as, upon becoming Emperor, he renounced Christianity and then, in a rather unchristian way, failed to murder and persecute his religious opponents. His attempt to restore the old religions was curtailed by his death in battle in Persia. The Christian Church survived to libel him with the dying words *'Vicisti, Galilean'* ('Thou hast conquered, O Galilean'), which were wished on him by Theodoret (386–*c.* 457), Bishop of Cyrrhus from 423.[245]

Juvenal, *see* John Milton

K

John F. Kennedy (1917–63), the thirty-fifth president of the United States, 1960–63). Anyone who ever heard a Kennedy speech – live, or on television or radio – knows why there was a magical aura to the brief Kennedy years. His oratory seemed to lift everyday words up to a nobler level. So when he said after the disastrous Bay of Pigs attempt to invade Cuba in April 1961 *'Victory has a hundred fathers but defeat is an orphan'*, it didn't matter that those exact words appeared in the diary of Count Ciano, Italian foreign minister under his father-in-law, Mussolini (*'La vittoria trova cento padri, e nessuno vuole riconoscere l'insuccesso'*)[246] published in America, in English, in 1946.

Kennedy had wit and was brave enough to use it, despite the readiness of opponents to respond with humourless outrage. Accused of buying votes, he told a Washington meeting: 'I have just received a telegram from my generous daddy: "Dear Jack, Don't buy a single vote more than necessary. I'll be damned if I'm going to pay for a land-

83

slide".'[247] Asked how he became a war hero: 'It was involuntary. They sank my boat.'[248]

Joseph P. Kennedy, *see* Knute Rockne

John Maynard Keynes, Baron Keynes, (1883–1946), the great economist.

Among much else, Keynes is remembered for '*Gold is a barbarous relic.*' Gold retains its allure for mankind for a host of reasons that need to be explained as much by a psychologist as by an economist. Keynes, the most worldly and commercial of economists, knew this. What he wrote was: 'In truth the gold **standard** is a barbarous relic.'[249] At the Bretton Woods conference in 1944 Keynes helped replace the gold standard, against which currencies fluctuated, with a system of fixed exchange rates. Paradoxically the new system only worked so long as America remained on the gold standard, and when in 1968 President Nixon took America off the gold standard the Bretton Woods system collapsed. The world could even return to a gold standard one day 'because people would rather trust a dead metal than a live politican' (trad.). *See also*, Stanley Baldwin, David Lloyd George *and* Lenin.

Lord and Lady Killearn, *see* Traditional

Rudyard Kipling (1865–1936), literary cheer-leader for the British Empire.

Generations of Englishmen were brought up on Kipling's stories and narrative poems. These, set largely in India, glorified the God-given duty of the English race* to rule

---

* An oxymoron, like 'thoroughbred mongrel'.

the world — or at least those bits of it without the military ability to stop them. On a contemporary scale of political incorrectness, Kipling must score 100 per cent — far worse, I imagine, than the likes of [Ex] Field-Marshal Idi Amin Dada or His [Ex] Imperial Majesty The Emperor Bokassa. *The Green Eye of the Yellow God*, ideal for declaiming in the village hall, is typical of Kipling's work . . .

> *There's a one-eyed yellow idol to the north of Katmandu*
> *There's a little marble cross below the town.*
> *There's a broken-hearted woman tends the grave of Mad Carew*
> *And the Yellow God forever gazes down.*

. . . apart from being written by Milton J. Hayes in 1911.

Kipling's view was, no doubt, influenced by the sort of English textbook his mother might have read, such as *The Young Woman's Companion* of 1814. The description of the English cannot be bettered as a piece of balanced, objective and factual reporting: 'The English are esteemed handsome in their persons, lovers of liberty, valiant in war, industrious in the arts of peace and extremely enterprising and active but reserved in their manners.' With the War of 1812† still fresh in English minds, the author took a jaundiced view of our American cousins: 'The inhabitants of the United States are both proud and ignorant; but frugal, industrious and warmly attached to liberty.'[250] Fourteen years later, in *The Young Man's Companion*, the description of Americans reflected the natural affinity between the two peoples. 'The inhabitants are famed for their ardent love of freedom, for their hospitality and industry, and for the great attention they pay to

† This is the war English schoolchildren are never told much about, if anything, because England lost.

[handwritten annotation:] Lost? The British burnt Washington — the Yanks ran away. American war aim was to incorporate Canada. Britain ceded no territory when the Yanks made peace. They lost!

agriculture and commerce.'[251] *See also* Kipling's first cousin, Stanley Baldwin, *and* Winston L. S. Churchill.

Captain James T. Kirk, Starfleet Commander, Starship Enterprise (1966–8).

Though it break a million Trekkies' hearts, in none of seventy-eight episodes of the original series did Captain Kirk (William Shatner) say '*Beam me up, Scotty*', only: 'Beam us up, Mr Scott', in 'Gamesters of Triskelion'. (A triskelion is a symbolic figure consisting of three legs radiating from a common centre.) If it be any consolation, Mr Spock (Leonard Nimoy) muttered 'Highly illogical' innumerbale times.[252]

In the original *Star Trek* series, the motto of the Enterprise was the now unacceptable 'To boldly go where no man has gone before.' But with *Star Trek – The Next Generation*, the series has become the very pineapple of political correctness[253] with the motto becoming: 'To boldy go where no one has gone before.'

Henry A. Kissinger (1923–), one-time American Secreatary of State, never said anything memorable, so Ronald Reagan and others made good the deficiency.

Reagan was a master of the art of eliding false opinions into the lexicon of his political opponents. In 1976 he said that Kissinger '. . . is quoted as saying that *he thinks of the United States as Athens and the Soviet Union as Sparta.*' Needless to say, the 'is quoted as saying that' didn't get much emphasis, but the second half of the quotation did. Kissinger said no such thing and furiously denied having done so. Since Athens was the cradle of democracy and learning, and, ultimately, triumphed over the military state of Sparta, it is hard to see what the fuss was about. This reasonable, albeit debatable, comment was actually made by Admiral Elmo R.

Zumwalt, American Chief of Naval Operations from 1970 to 1974.

That same year in a television interview Reagan quoted Kissinger as saying: '*The day of the United States is past and today is the day of the Soviet Union . . . My job as Secretary of State is to negotiate the most acceptable second-best position.*'[254] That is pure invention – and what do you conclude about a man who would invent, or repeat, such a quote and a public who would belive it? *See also* Francis I.

Monseigneur Ronald Knox, *see* Queen Victoria

L

Henry Labouchère, *see* Benjamin Disraeli

Fiorello La Guardia, *see* Mark Twain

Alan Ladd, *see* John Wayne

Charles Lamb (1775–1834), wit, writer and critic, friend of Wordsworth, Southey and Coleridge, best known for his *Essays of Elia*.

Lamb was no favourite of Mr Hesketh Pearson, who wrote of his use of the phrase '*Neat not gaudy*' against Shakespeare's 'Rich not gaudy' in *Hamlet*, that: 'Charles Lamb was the first to bleat forth this meaningless version of a good phrase and his devotees have followed him like sheep.'[255] Lamb was not the first to use the phrase, as the Revd Samuel Wesley (1662–1735) wrote: 'Style is the dress of thought; a modest dress, Neat, but not gaudy, will the true critic please.'[256] Secondly, Lamb's use of the phrase was, in context, unexceptionable. 'A little thin flowery border round, neat not gaudy.'[257]

Mr Pearson is not to be criticized. It may be that not every hint of prejudice has been eliminated from the text of this book.

William Lamb (Viscount Melbourne), *see* Benjamin Disraeli

Louis L'Amour, *see* John Wayne

Sir Miles and Lady Lampson, *see* Traditional

Robert or William Langland, *see* Aesop

Stan Laurel, *see* – of course – Oliver Hardy

(Andrew) Bonar Law (1858–1923), statesman and British prime minister, 1922–3, was said to have excused a poor decision with: '*I must follow them. I am their leader.*'[258]

Bonar Law is unjustly judged by his premiership, throughout which he was slowly dying of cancer of the throat, and was not the incisive leader of steely personality he had been in his prime. If he ever made this uncharacteristic quip – and it is unlikely he did – he was paraphrasing Alexandre Ledru-Rollin, a French liberal surveying the mob fighting at the Paris barricades during the 1848 revolution. 'Oh well! I am their leader, I really ought to follow them.' ('*Eh! Je suis leur chef, il fallait bien les suivre.*')[259] Or Law may have been thinking of Gilbert and Sullivan's Duke of Plaza-Toro: 'In enterprise of martial kind/When there was any fighting/He led his regiment from behind/He found it less exciting.'[260]

'*Intelligent people and intelligence bear the same relationship as gentlemen and gents.*'[261] This has been attributed to Law, to Lord Birkenhead and to Stanley Baldwin, who actually said: 'The word intelligentsia always seems to me to bear the same relation to intelligence as the word gent does to gentleman.'[262]

Alexandre Ledru-Rollin, *see* A. Bonar Law

Leiber and Stoller, *see* Edward Bulwer Lytton

Lenin (Vladimir Ilich Ulyanov (1870–1924), proto-Marxist-Leninist. Lenin is the Communist arch-villain to whom John Birchers and others 'slightly to the right of Ghengis Khan' ascribe fake quotations – in preference to Marx or Stalin. The following is a cross-section from a wide choice.[263]

'*The best way to destroy capitalism is to debauch the currency. By a continuing process of inflation, government can confiscate, secretly and unobserved, an important part of the wealth of their citizens.*' John Maynard Keynes wrote: 'Lenin was right. There is no subtler, no surer means of overturning the existing basis of society than to debauch the currency.'[264] But Keynes prefaced his comment with: 'Lenin . . . is said to have declared that . . .', and no earlier record of Lenin's alleged words can be found.

Nor did Lenin say '*The capitalists will sell us the rope with which to hang them.*' Nor: '*Corrupt the young people of a nation and the battle is won.*' Nor: '*Promises are like pie-crust, made to be broken.*'

The following nonsense is still ascribed to Lenin by fanatics from the National Rifle Association of America. '*The first step to overthrowing a government is to establish a firearms registration law. After gaining sufficient strength, charge a suspected conspiracy, confiscate the weapons, and you will have neutralized the defence of the people.'* America is the only country in the world where the ownership of non-sporting firearms is common. Such a 'first step' would never have occurred to Lenin.

Sidney and Beatrice Webb, of the soft rather than the hard Left, attribute to Lenin: *'It is true that liberty is precious — so precious it must be rationed'*, but this sentiment, so useful to the far Right, has no other ancestry than these dubious parents.[265]

Democracy and freedom have no need of such spurious quotations and are not helped by rabid right-wingers descending to the propaganda techniques of Josef Goebbels. *See also* A. J. Cook.

Abraham Lincoln (1809–65), sixteenth president of the United States from 1861 until his assassination in 1865.

The Great Emancipator, a secular saint, has been recruited to many unlikely causes by the means of fake quotations. He has supported Mussolini's right to the entire Dalmatian coast; while voicing his total belief in Christianity he has also attacked the unsoundness of the Christian scheme of salvation; he has damned Prohibition in intemperate terms, taken a pure Marxist view on the value of labour, called baseball essential for the well-being of the country and paraphrased Professor J. K. Galbraith in condemning the power of the big corporations.[266]

Typical is the strongly protectionist statement in favour of high tariff walls to keep out cheap foreign goods. 'When an American paid twenty dollars for steel rails to an English manufacturer, America had the steel and England had the twenty dollars. But when he paid twenty dollars for the steel to an American manufacturer, America had both the steel and the twenty dollars.' When you learn that these words appeared in a New York weekly, *American Protectionist*, on 29 June 1894, it is no surprise the quotation is spurious. Lincoln died two weeks before the first rails were ever rolled in America.

Nor did Lincoln say: '*Here I stand — warts and all*', nor '*God must have loved the common people; he made so many of them.*' Nor did he write the great credo of the moderate Right:

> *You cannot bring about prosperity by discouraging thrift.*
> *You cannot strengthen the weak by weakening the strong.*
> *You cannot help strong men by tearing down big men.*
> *You cannot help the wage-earner by pulling down the wage-payer.*
> *You cannot further the brotherhood of man by encouraging class hatred.*
> *You cannot help the poor by destroying the rich.*
> *You cannot establish sound security on borrowed money.*
> *You cannot keep out of trouble by spending more than you earn.*
> *You cannot build character and courage by taking away a man's initiative.*
> *You cannot help men permanently by doing for them what they could and should do for themselves.*

Those words appeared on the verso of a 1942 handbill headed 'Lincoln on Limitations', and credited 'Inspiration of William J. H. Boetcker', who was a Presbyterian minister. Since they sounded far more impressive as a Lincoln quote than a Boetcker quote, a Lincoln quote they became.[267]

Lincoln, the advocate of self-respect and self-reliance, often urged the people '*Paddle your own canoe*', but the British writer, Captain (Frederick) Marryat used it in 1844 in his book *The Settlers in Canada*. Let's call it a draw. *See also* Phineas T. Barnum.

David Lloyd George, *see* (correctly) *under* George

John Locke, *see* Thomas Jefferson

Alice Roosevelt Longworth (1884–1980), daughter of President Theodore Roosevelt, had a nice line in cushions, one of which had embroidered upon it, 'If you haven't anything nice to say about anyone, come and sit by me.'[268]

Mrs Longworth acted as a clearing-house for all the Washington gossip, and many of her best *bons mots* weren't hers, although she did call her cousin, Franklin Delano Roosevelt, 'one third sap and two-thirds Eleanor'. When she said of Thomas Dewey, the vertically underprivileged governor of New York: '*How can the Republican Party nominate a man who looks like the bridegroom – on a wedding cake?*' she was quoting another Washington socialite, Grace Hodgson Flandrau.[269] *See also* Calvin Coolidge.

Louis XIV King of France (1638–1715), lived in an age when, even in France, most people believed in the divine right of kings. So for Louis, an absolute monarch, to say '*L'état, c'est moi*' – 'The state is me', or 'I am the state', was just a pithy statement of the obvious.

With all his faults, Louis was not given to trite remarks and there is no evidence he ever uttered these words – he didn't need to – although when later attributed to him, the occasions given were detailed: before the Parliament of Paris on 13 April 1655 and at Court, 'Louis interrupted a judge who used the expression "The king and the state" by saying "I am the state".'[270] Both spurious ascriptions probably stem from the diktat Louis did use. 'The nation does not form a corporate entity in France; it exists fully and completely, in the person of the king.' ('*La nation ne fait pas corps en France: elle réside tout entière dans la personne du roi.*')[271]

On the other hand, Napoleon Bonaparte (q.v.), self-proclaimed emperor, did need to say so. 'What is the throne? A bit of wood gilded and covered in velvet. I am the state. I alone am here representative of the people.'[272]

When in 1700 Louis's seventeen-year-old grandson, Philippe duc d'Anjou, left Paris to become King of Spain, his grandfather is credited by Voltaire with saying *'The Pyrenees no longer exist'* (*'Il n'y a plus de Pyrénées'*). However the *Mercure Galant* of that November credits the Spanish ambassador with the comment, and this is confirmed by the diary of the Marquis de Dangeau.[273]

James Russell Lowell (1819–91), American ambassador to Britain and poet, gave us that invaluable line *'Enough to make a saint swear'*, but the whole point about saints is they are so above the mortal ills of this world that nothing should make them swear. What Lowell wrote – far more true but far less theatrical – was 'Enough to make a deacon swear.'[274]

St Ignatius de Loyola (1491–1556), founder of the Society of Jesus, better known as the Jesuits, in 1539.

The Jesuits have always placed great stress on intellectual calibre and rigorous self-discipline. This has not endeared them to the majority who lack the former and are incapable of the latter. Hence St Ignatius's sinister and best-known saying is: *'Give me a boy until he is seven and he is ours for life.'* What he actually said was: 'Give me a boy until he is seven and I will show you a man.'

Edward Bulwer Lytton, 2nd Baron and 1st Earl of Lytton (1805–73), politician, Member of Parliament, Colonial Secretary, baronet and peer. Edward George Bulwer Lytton was a prodigious literary figure as well.

In Lytton's play *Richelieu* (1839), the timeless 'Beneath the rule of men entirely great, *the pen is mightier than the sword*' was born, or reinterpreted. For in his preface to the *Anatomy of Melancholy*, 'Democritus to the Reader' (1621), Robert Burton writes: '*Hic quam sit calamus saevior ense patet*', or 'From this it is clear how much the pen is worse than the sword.'[275] More modern variations include Leiber and Stoller's 'The pen is mightier than the sword but no match for a gun.'[276] Mr Burton, no doubt, rolls over and over in his grave.

Lytton has been given credit for '*Chickens come home to roost*', but his original was more interesting: 'Curses are like young chickens, And still come home to roost.' But he is only the publicist for the phrase, the full verse being:

Curse away!
And let me tell thee, Beauseant,
a wise proverb
The Arabs have – 'Curses are like
young chickens,
And still come home to roost'[277]

Robert Southey used the phrase in 1810 in *The Curse of Kehama*.

Curses have an inbuilt thirst for publicity and, public or private, never seem to do their authors any good.

M

General Douglas MacArthur (1880–1964), Field Marshal of the Philippine army and later Second World War commander of Allied forces in the Pacific.

MacArthur was defending the Philippines in 1942 but fled to Australia ahead of the advancing Japanese forces. Arriving in Australia on 20 March, he made some off-the-cuff remarks to the waiting journalists. '*The President of the United States ordered me to break through the Japanese lines and proceed from Corregidor to Australia for the purpose ... of organizing the American offensive against Japan. A primary purpose of this is relief of the Philippines. I came through and I shall return.*' Those last three words, '*I shall return*' contributed greatly to the Mac-Arthur myth but they were not the spontaneous comment you would believe from MacArthur's *Reminiscences*, nor were they MacArthur's words. The statement had been prepared by MacArthur's staff before he escaped and, as agreed, was broadcast in the Philippines by Colonel Carlos Romulo as soon as he heard MacArthur was safely in Australia.[278]

MacArthur was appointed by President Franklin Roosevelt who said of him: 'Never underestimate a man who overestimates himself.' He was sacked by President Truman who explained: 'I fired him because he wouldn't respect the authority of the President. I didn't fire him because he was a dumb son of a bitch, although he was, but that's not against the law in generals. If it was, half to three-quarters of them would be in jail.' A third president, General Dwight D. Eisenhower, was disdainful: 'Oh yes. I studied dramatics under him for twelve years.'[279]

After Truman sacked MacArthur he allowed the general one last address to the Joint Houses of Congress. In it, MacArthur voiced the sentiment *'Old soldiers never die. They just fade away.'* This was not his, but the title of a 1920 song by J. Foley. The original line was 'Kind thoughts can never die'.[280]

Thomas Babington Macaulay (1st Baron Macaulay, 1800–59), infant prodigy, 'a book in breeches', writer, lawyer, politician.[281]

Macaulay, blessed with a photographic memory and total recall, often scorned less fortunate mortals. His claim 'Every schoolboy knows . . .' has entered the language, done arduous duty and been pensioned off as a cliché. But few remember the rest of the sentence, required for a proper appreciation of Macaulay. 'Every schoolboy knows who imprisoned Montezuma, and who strangled Atahualpa.' The answers, probably unknown to 999 schoolboys in 1,000, are Hernando Cortez and Francisco Pizarro. Macaulay is always credited with the avowal, but a century earlier Jonathan Swift wrote:

> How haughtily he cocks his nose
> To tell what every schoolboy knows.[282]

While a century before him, Bishop Jeremy Taylor wrote: 'Every schoolboy knows it.'[283]

The diarrhoea suffered by so many visitors to Mexico is 'Montezuma's revenge'. *See also* Edmund Burke *and* Benjamin Disraeli.

Senator Joseph McCarthy, *see* Robert G. Ingersoll *and* Thomas Jefferson

William Topaz McGonagall, *see* Alfred Austin

Iain Macleod, *see* 5th Marquess of Salisbury

(Maurice) Harold Macmillan, (1st Earl of Stockton, 1894–1986), statesman and British prime minister, 1957–63, who won the 1959 general election with the help of the suggestion, *'You've never had it so good.'*

Speaking at Bedford on 20 July 1957 the prime minister said: 'Let's be frank about it; most of our people have never had it so good . . . What is beginning to worry some of us is "Is it too good to be true", or perhaps I should say, "Is it too good to last?"'[284] A far cry from the popular contraction which was a Democratic Party slogan in the 1952 American election campaigns. Macmillan always projected an ebullient image and that roistering paraphrase helped 'SuperMac' win the general election two years later. He never much objected to being so usefully misquoted.

Macmillan had a style and panache which none of his successors has matched. In 1958 his entire Treasury team of three ministers resigned, but unflappable Mac just referred to the matter as 'these little local difficulties' (usually misquoted in the singular), appointed their successors and set off as planned on his extended tour of the Commonwealth. In full: 'I thought the best thing to do was to settle up these little local difficulties, and then to turn to the wider vision of the Commonwealth.'[285] In those days, Her Majesty the Queen was not the only person left in the world who cherished the Commonwealth.

Another famous speech was delivered to the South African parliament on 3 February 1960. *'The wind of change is blowing through this continent. Whether we like it or not, this growth of political consciousness is a political fact.'* That was written for Macmillan by a civil servant, Sir David Hunt, but it was first used, less ambiguously, by Stanley Baldwin on 4 December 1934: 'There is a wind of nationalism and freedom blowing around the world.'[286] *See also* 5th Marquess of Salisbury, Richard Brinsley Sheridan *and* Stanley Baldwin.

Captain William A. Maguire (1890–1953) was a US navy chaplain at the time of the Japanese attack on Pearl Harbor on 7 December 1941.

Captain Maguire's rallying cry on that ill-fated day rang around the world: '*Praise the Lord and pass the ammunition.*' Or was it that of another naval chaplain, Lieutenant Howell Forgey? Or neither? Or nobody? Father Maguire said that 'If I said it nobody could have heard me in the din of battle.' Whatever the truth the cry helped morale, especially after Frank Loesser put the words to music. The song became one of the hits of the Second World War. The Maguire/Forgey rallying cry is older than either of them, having been traced back to the American Civil War, and it may be even earlier.[287]

Ern Malley (1919–44) was, briefly, one of the giants of Australian modern poetry shortly after his untimely demise in 1944 aged only twenty-five.

Malley's reputation was established after his sister, Ethel, sent some of his poems to Max Harris, editor of the self-consciously modernistic down-under literary journal *Angry Penguins*. Malley's poems, such as *Culture And Exhibit*, received ecstatic appreciation.

> Swamps, marshes, barrowpits and other
> Areas of stagnant water serve
> As breeding grounds

Malleys' reputation was further enhanced when one of his poems in *Angry Penguins* was deemed obscene, and Harris was fined five pounds for publishing it. Critical opinion turned mute when it was learned that Ern Malley was the pen-name of two bored servicemen, Lieutenant James MacAuley and Corporal Harold Stewart, who concocted Malley's 'poetry' from anything available. *Culture And Exhibit* was lifted, verbatim, from an American booklet on mosquito control.[288]

It is easy to spot the counterfeit when comparing Mr Malley's work to the real thing.

> All children are small and crusty
> And all pale, blind, humble waters are cleaning.
> A insect, dumb and torrid, comes of the daddyo
> How is an insect into this fur?[289]

That miniature masterpiece *Auto-Beatnik Poem No 41: Insects* was written in 1961 at the dawning of the age of flower-power innocence. It remains as strikingly modern now as it was then.

Sir John Manderville, *see* Aesop

Herman Mankiewicz, *see* Winston L. S. Churchill

Joseph L. Mankiewicz, *see* Spencer Tracy

Sir Reginald Manningham-Buller, *see* Traditional

Mao Zedong, *see* Karl von Clausewitz

Senator William L. Marcy, *see* Andrew Jackson

Marie-Antoinette (1755–93), Queen of France, guillotined after the French Revolution. History is written by the victors, which is why Marie-Antoinette's best-known utterance is her response when told that the peasants had no bread to eat: 'Qu'ils mangent de la brioche?' – 'Why don't they eat cake?' (not *Let them eat cake*'). She neither asked nor quoted that ingenuous question.

The philosopher Jean-Jacques Rousseau refers in his *Confessions* to '. . . the thoughtless saying of a great princess who, on being informed that the country people had no bread, replied "Let them eat cake".'[290] But they were published in 1778, some years before Marie-Antoinette was alleged to have asked her question – and less well-documented sources have it even earlier.

'Groucho' (Julius Henry) Marx (1890–1977), American comedian.

Groucho's one foray into politics, *'This country would be all right if Truman were alive*'[291] (sometimes '. . . *if Truman were President*') was made in 1947 when the thirty-third president was still very much animate. Groucho later denied the witticism, but how can you trust a man who said in *A Day at the Races* (1937), 'Either he's dead or my watch has stopped.'?[292]

Marx's political thinking attracted followers of many kinds. In England some were of the militant tendency; in France some would proudly state: *'Je suis Marxiste – tendance Groucho.'*[293]

Karl Marx (1818–83), like all great prophets (true and false), was wildly misinterpreted by his disciples for their own benefit.

He did not say *'Property is theft.'* Pierre Joseph Proudhon made the remark in 1840, 'La propriété c'est le vol.'[294] With his modest private income, Marx was all in favour of a modest degree of private property.

Marx's comment '*History repeats itself; the first time as tragedy, the second as farce*' is a bad précis. What Marx said was: 'Hegel says somewhere that all great events and personalities in world history reappear in one fashion or another. He forgot to add: the first time as tragedy, the second as farce.'[295] Charles Wolf Jr. explained why the second time is farce: 'Those who don't study the past will repeat its errors: those who do will find other ways to err.'[296]

Sir James Matthew, *see* Anatole France

Viscount Melbourne (William Lamb), *see* Benjamin Disraeli

Sir James Melville (1535–1617), man of affairs, wrote of carrying 'Coals to Newcastle' in his autobiography, but the first half of the phrase has been forgotten: 'Salt to Dysart or Coals to Newcastle'. The French speak of carrying water to the river (*porter de l'eau à la rivière*), the Romans talked of carrying wood to the forest and the Greeks, more picturesquely, of sending owls to Athens.

When Sir Samuel Hoare Bt. was forced to resign as British Foreign Secretary over the Hoare–Laval Pact in December 1935, he had to return his seals of office to the King. George V said: 'No more coals to Newcastle, no more Hoares to Paris, eh!' which did not amuse the prim Sir Samuel as much as it did his tactless monarch.

H. L. Mencken, *see* Rupert Murdoch

Thomas Middleton, *see* William Shakespeare

Sir Ronald Millar, *see* Margaret Thatcher

Joe Miller (1684–1738) was an actor who died leaving his family in poverty.

Miller had nothing to do with writing the long-famous *Joe Miller's Jest Book*, the first anthology of jokes to appear in English. It was compiled by his friend John Mottley, the playwright, as a benefit for Miller's wife and family. The original book contained only 272 jokes, expanded in subsequent editions to over 1,500. The real joke is not only that Miller was illiterate, but that he was also a grave and silent man, never given to jesting.[297]

John Milton (1608–74), is a poet more quoted than read.

Milton's best-known adage is '*Revenge is sweet*', but his actual lines were: 'Revenge at first though sweet/Bitter ere long back on itself recoils.'[298] Poets and thinkers are divided on revenge. Only a few echo the old Spanish proverb 'Revenge is a dish best enjoyed cold' with, for example, Emile Gaboriau's 'Revenge is a luscious fruit which you must leave to ripen', or Pierre Corneille's 'Just vengeance does not call for punishment.' Some take the neutral middle ground as do Heraclitus: 'It is difficult to fight against anger, for a man will buy revenge with his soul', and Charles Caleb Colton: 'Revenge is a much more punctual paymaster than gratitude.' Most, however, take a high moral tone. Juvenal wrote: 'Revenge is always the joy of narrow, sick and petty minds.' The great Bacon (Francis, not Roger) opined: 'In taking revenge a man is but even with his enemy; but in passing it over he is superior.'[299]

Addison Mizner (1872–1933), American architect. Way before the giddy days of Prohibition, Mizner took some liberties with St Paul's Epistle to the Romans (4:23) by writing, 'The wages of gin is breath.' which appeared in the immensely popular *Cynic's Calendar* (1901). Addison's brother, Wilson Mizner, was a member of the Algonquin Round Table and the better-known wit of the two.

General Emilio Mola, *see* General Francisco Franco

Charles Montague, *see* William Congreve

Casimir, Comte de Montrond, *see* John Dryden

Caroline Moore, *see* Val Hennessy

Julia Moore, *see* Alfred Austin

Thomas Moore, *see* Richard Brinsley Sheridan

General George Pope Morris, (1802–64), American soldier and poet.

Morris has taken the credit for the once sickeningly sentimental, now ecologically lauded, doggerel with the title and refrain '*Woodman, Spare that Tree*' . . .

> Woodman, spare that tree!
> Touch not a single bough
> In youth it sheltered me,
> And I'll protect it now.[300]

. . . published in 1830. Twenty-three years earlier Thomas Campbell wrote *The Beech Tree's Petition*.

> Here on my trunk's surviving frame
> Carved many a long forgotten name . . .
> As Love's own alter, honor me:
> Spare woodman, spare the beechen tree.[301]

The smooth bark of the beech was much used by lovers wishing to carve their initials upon a tree. Earlier the outer and inner bark of the beech was used by the Anglo-Saxon scribes as parchment. They called the beech, and its bark, 'boc', from which comes the word 'book'.

Marion Michael Morrison, *see* John Wayne

Samuel Finlay Breese Morse (1791–1872) deftly patented the telegraph invented by his mentor, Professor Joseph Henry of Princeton, and filched the credit for the idea, too.

When Congress voted him $30,000 to perfect 'his idea', he laid a wire between Washington and Baltimore and famously sent the world's first telegraph message, '*What God hath wrought.*' And very proper too. The actual message, 'Everything worked well', was far too prosaic for so momentous an event.[302]

John Mottley, *see* Joe Miller

Baron Karl Frederich Hieronymous von Munchhausen (1720–97), was a boastful German officer in the Russian army.

In his later years Baron Munchhausen (count the h's) would tell the tales from *Baron Munchhausen's Narrative of His Marvellous Travels and Campaigns in Russia*. By the time he died, Munchhausen happily believed they had all happened to him – but he did not even write them. The author of the stories, first published anonymously in London in 1785, was a German-born Dutch intellectual, petty criminal, mining engineer and confidence trickster, one Rudolf Eric Raspe (1734–94). The stories were, in part, a satire on such travelogues as those by Baron de Tott and James Bruce, who discovered the source of the Blue Nile. (Bruce's factual *Travels in Abyssinia*, considered so outrageous as to be thought fiction, was not, as stated by Brewer, a source for *Munchausen* as it was published five years later.) Raspe deserves to be remembered for *Munchausen* but, if remembered at all, it will be for swindling Sir John Sinclair and thus becoming the model for the dastardly Herman Dousterswivel in Sir Walter Scott's *The Antiquary* (1816).[303]

(Keith) Rupert Murdoch (1931–), a latter-day mixture of Lord Northcliffe and William Randolph Hearst. Global media mogul.

When Murdoch bought the *Sun* from IPC in 1969 it appeared to be losing money on a vast scale. He was the only man who realized it wasn't. Most of those losses were the paper's share of the heavy IPC head-office overheads. Murdoch immediately took the *Sun* downmarket on the grounds: *'Nobody ever lost money underestimating the public taste'* – a offence of which the paper has never since been guilty. If Murdoch ever used those words he was paraphrasing H. L. Mencken. 'No one in this world, so far as I know . . . has ever lost money by underestimating the intelligence of the great masses of the plain people.'[304] The *Sun* has been highly profitable since shortly after Murdoch bought it, and its cash flow funded most of his subsequent expansion programme.

Benito Mussolini (1883–1945), Italian Fascist dictator, 1922–43. During the Second World War, Mussolini was presented by Allied propaganda as Hitler's jackal and a blustering buffoon. But *Il Duce* was not thought a joke before the War. Winston Churchill wrote: 'It would be a dangerous folly for the British people to underrate the enduring position in world history which Mussolini will hold; or the amazing qualities of courage, comprehension, self-control and perseverance which he exemplifies.'[305]

Mussolini saw himself as in the tradition of the warrior statesmen of ancient Rome. '*Meglio vivere un giorno da leone che cent'anni da pecora.*' ('I would rather be a lion for a day than a sheep for a century.') '*Se avanzo seauitemi, se indietreggio uccidetemi.*' ('If I advance follow me. If I retreat kill me.') The first comment was a well-known piece of graffiti from the Great War and the second was pinched from Garibaldi,[306] and he took it from the Vendean hero, the Marquis de La Rochejaquelein (1777–1815), whose original is the most elegant: 'We go to meet the foe. If I advance follow me. If I retreat slay me. If I fall avenge me.'[307]

N

General Sir Charles Napier (1782–1853), soldier. In 1841 Sir Charles was sent to India to command British troops in the war against the Amir of Sind (now part of Pakistan). Two years later, against far superior forces, he gained a great victory at Mecanee and then took the capital, Hyderabad, conquering the province. He sent a laconic telegram in Latin to Lord Ellenborough, the Governor-General of India: '*Peccavi*' – I have sinned.

Sadly this charming pun was not sent by Napier to

Ellenborough but by Catherine Winkworth to *Punch*, which published it on 18 May 1844.[308]

Napoleon I (Napoleon Bonaparte, 1769–1821), French general, consul, emperor 1804–15 and ex-emperor.

With a genius for appropriation, whether other people's countries or wives, it should come as no surprise that although Bonaparte got some mileage out of '*L'Angleterre est une nation de boutiquiers*', or in the even more insulting translation: 'England is a nation of shopkeepers', he was not its originator. In *Wealth of Nations* (1776), Adam Smith observed that 'To found a great empire for the sole purpose of raising up a people of customers, may at first sight appear a project fit only for a nation of shopkeepers. It is, however, a project altogether unfit for a nation of shopkeepers; but extremely fit for a nation that is governed by shopkeepers.' Which only proves that the English tend to theorize about nations of shopkeepers, rather than actually aspiring to be one.[309] It is unlikely that Napoleon was quoting Adam Smith, but he may well have known of Bertrand Barère's speech on 11 June 1794: 'Let Pitt then boast of his victory to his nation of shopkeepers.'[310]

Bonaparte is not the father of: '*God is always on the side of the big battalions*', but only the step-father – as are most great generals, all of whom have noticed this little idiosyncrasy of the Almighty's. The earliest record of the sentiment is from Tacitus (*c.* 55–120): '*Deus fortioribus adesse*' which, being Latin, is the pithiest. Bussy-Rabutin[311] was more exact, but verbose: '*Dieu est d'ordinaire pour les gros escadrons contre les petits*', or 'God is normally for the big battalions against the small ones.' Frederick the Great echoed: '*Dieu est pour les gros escadrons*', and so have many other soldiers at different times and in different languages.[312] Frederick's adviser, Voltaire, cautiously prefaced the remark with the caveat 'On dit que ...' ('It is said that ...').[313] Oliver Cromwell (q.v.) took a similarly prosaic view on keeping one's powder dry. God's partisanship was not restricted to land; Gibbon noted: 'The winds and waves are always on the side of the ablest navigators.'[314] Damon Runyon expressed the same sentiment differently: 'The race is not always to the swift nor the battle to the strong – but that's the way to bet.'

Bonaparte did refer to 'La perfide Albion' – 'Perfidious Albion'*[315] in 1803, but the sentiment had been popular in France long before his time, as it remains to this day. In 1792 the Marquis de Ximinez said: 'Attaquons dans ses eaux, la perfide Albion',[316] or 'Let us attack in her own waters perfidious Albion.' Over a century earlier, Jacques-Bernigne Bossuet (1627–1704) in a sermon at Metz, said: 'England, ah perfidious England, which the protection afforded by its seas rendered inaccessible to the Romans, the faith of the Saviour spread even there.'[317] ('L'Angleterre, ah la perfide Angleterre, que le rempart de ses mers rendoit inaccessible aux romains, la foi du Sauveur y est abordée.') For some unfathomable reason the British seem smugly proud of this French attitude.

In 1812 after his retreat from Moscow Bonaparte told the Polish ambassador 'From the sublime to the ridiculous is but a small step' ('Du sublime au ridicule il n'y a qu'un pas')[318], but Tom Paine (1737–1809) had the idea first. 'The sublime and the ridiculous are often so nearly related, that it is difficult to class them separately. One step above the sublime, makes the ridiculous; and one step above the ridiculous makes the sublime again.'[319] Harry Graham expressed the same thought differently:[320]

* 'Beyond the Pillars of Hercules is the ocean that flows round the earth, and in it are two very large islands called Britannia, vis. Albion and Ierne.'

Aunt Jane observed, the second time
   She tumbled off a bus,
'The step is short from the Sublime
   To the Ridiculous'.

See also Lord Byron, Charles de Gaulle, Robert G. Ingersoll, King Louis XIV *and* Johnnie Ray.

Ogden Nash (1902–71), poet. '*Shake and shake the catsup bottle/None will come and then a lot'll*' – typical of Ogden Nash – is a fitting chaperon for such gems as: 'I could of, If I would of/But I shouldn't, So I douldn't', or: 'Who wants my jellyfish? I'm not sellyfish', and: 'I would live all my life in nonchalance and insouciance/Were it not for making a living, which is rather an nouciance.' The last three poems are by Nash but the first is by Richard Armour who suffers from having his work called 'whimsical'.[321]

The *News of the World* is the Sunday newspaper with the slogan '*All human life is there*', but it wasn't original to Maurice Smelt, the advertising copywriter who introduced it to the paper in the late 1950s. Henry James, the Anglo-American novelist, wrote in 1879: 'Cats and monkeys – monkeys and cats – all human life is there.'[322] The paper has never used the first half of James's sentence in its advertising.

Sir Isaac Newton (1642–1727), physicist and mathematician. '*If I have seen farther, it is by standing on the shoulders of giants.*' Newton was only the last in a long line of great men who have used this thought to put their own contributions into perspective. It appears in this form in a letter Newton wrote to Robert Hooke, a fellow physicist, in 1675/76, but is most surely derived from Robert Burton's *The Anatomy of*

Melancholy: 'Pygmies placed on the shoulders of giants see more than the giants themselves.' Burton himself had a little help from Bernard of Chartres (*c.* 1130) who said: 'We are like dwarfs on the shoulders of giants, so that we can see more than they, and things at a greater distance, not by virtue of any sharpness of sight on our part, or any physical distinction, but because we are carried high and raised up by their giant size.'[323]

Friedrich Wilhelm Nietzsche, *see* Voltaire

General Robert Nivelle, *see* (Henri) Philippe Pétain

Richard M. Nixon, *see* Lyndon B. Johnson *and* Francis I

Christopher North (the pen-name of John Wilson, 1785–1854), Scots poet and essayist.

'The Empire on which the sun never sets' typifies the high point of Victorian imperialism. Like so many Victorian attitudes it predated Victoria, who was more a follower than a leader of social opinion. Mr North wrote in 1829 of 'His Majesty's dominions, on which the sun never sets'. But Captain John Smith wrote in 1631: 'Why should the brave Spanish soldier brag the sun never sets in the Spanish dominions?' Philip II of Spain (1527–98) is the probable father of the concept 'the sun never sets on my dominions'[324].

It is, of course, well known that the sun never sets on the British Empire because the Almighty would not trust the British in the dark.

Viscount Norwich, *see Private Eye*

Ramon Novarro (1899–1968), star of the silent screen, was dropped by MGM, but not because his voice was wrong for the talkies nor because in *Mata Hari*, starring opposite Greta Garbo, he interpolated the line '*What's the matter, Mata?*': he didn't.

'MGM got rid of Novarro because he was homosexual and refused to marry a woman for publicity. Most of Garbo's great leading men were homosexual – and in getting rid of them MGM tried to make stars of dull men like Malvyn Douglas, and in the process they hurt Garbo and stripped her of that ethereal romance we loved.'[325]

'Bill' Nye, *see* Mark Twain

Frank Ward O'Malley (1875–1932), did not coin the aphorism '*Life is just one damn thing after another*', it was Elbert Hubbard (1856–1915) the American disciple of William Morris and founder of the Roycroft Press.[326] Edna St Vincent Millay's emendation was: 'It's not true that life is one damn thing after another – it's one damn thing over and over.'[327] At least both are less discouraging than 'Life's a bitch. And then you die' (trad.). Damon Runyon got the balance right: '"In fact", Sam the Gonoph says, "I long ago came to the conclusion that all life is six to five against."'[328]

The Caliph Omar (581–644), one of Muhammad's fathers-in-law. Conqueror of Persia, Syria, Palestine and Egypt. Assassinated.

Few acts are more horrifying than book-burning; few stories more horrible than the destruction of the great library at Alexandria. After Omar conquered the city he ordered General Amru to destroy the library as: '*All that men need to known is in this one book, the Holy Koran*', and the scrolls fuelled the furnaces of the public baths for six months. This great libel was put upon Omar by Abul-Faragius (or Bar Hebraeus), Bishop of Aleppo (1226–86), writing six centuries later. The libraries established by the Ptolemies (323–30 BC), the Brucheum and the Serapeum housing 700,000 scrolls, had already been despoiled by the time of the Saracen invasion of AD 640. The main library was destroyed during Caesar's wars of 48–47 BC, restored by Cleopatra and destroyed again by Aurelian in AD 273. Then 'In 389 or 391 an edict of Bishop Theodosius [ruler of Alexandria] ordered the destruction of the Serapeum, and its books were pillaged by the Christians.'[329] The early Church did not like other people's ideas – the later Church does not seem too keen on them either.

George Oppenheim, *see* Samuel Goldwyn

George Orwell(Eric Blair), *see* Julian called 'The Apostate'

James Otis (1725–83), American lawyer, gave the rallying cry that inspired the American War of Independence or the American Revolution – depending on which way you look at it.

'*Taxation without representation is tyranny*' has become as automatically accepted as has the right to self-determination and democracy. Putting to one side the interesting discussion that none of these ideas are absolutes, we should also put aside the idea that the first belongs to Otis. Indeed it cannot even be traced back to the eighteenth century, let alone 1761 and the Boston court where Otis is said to have used it. Its earliest recorded use is by America's second president, John Adams, in 1820.[330] The phrase is a splendid afterthought, justifying the War of Independence. Nobody thought of it at the time as, even in England, the parliamentary franchise was restricted to about one household in twenty and this was considered unremarkable.

Nor was the American War of Independence about taxation. As the erudite Iowan, Bill Bryson, notes: 'In the 1760s, it was estimated, the average American paid about sixpence a year in tax. The average Briton paid twenty-five shillings – fifty times as much. And in any case, Americans seldom actually paid their taxes. The hated Townsend duties raised just £259 in revenue in their first year and cost £170,000 to implement. The equally reviled Stamp Act duties were never collected at all.'[331] Neither was the War about freedom and human rights. When the American Declaration of Independence talked of all men being created equal it did not mean all men but all free men. As Dr Johnson (q.v.) noted: 'How is it we hear the loudest yelps for liberty among the drivers of Negroes?'[332]

The *Farmers' Almanac* observed: 'If James Otis thought taxation without representation was bad, he should see how bad it is *with* representation.'[333]

The Oxford Union. On 9 February 1933 the Union caused a great furore by passing a motion reported by Winston Churchill[334] as: *'That this House refuses to fight for king and country'*: the King and Country debate. The result was 275 votes in favour and 153 against, a majority of 122.[335] Ideas are the most powerful force in politics, and the idea arose that the coming generation of the nation's best brains and future leaders was turning pacifist. Michael Foot, later the leader of the Labour Party, expressed the view of the students: 'If peace is to be placed first, appeals to fight in the name of king and country cannot be allowed to intervene.'[336]

The actual motion, written by the Union's then librarian, D. M. Graham, was: 'This House will in no circumstances fight for its king and country' – unequivocal, more serious and more worrying for the prime minister of the time, Stanley Baldwin, fighting to persuade Britain to rearm. Curiously Churchill quotes the motion correctly in the UK edition of his book, *The Gathering Storm*, but incorrectly in the later American edition. No doubt he had his reasons.

P

Thomas Paine, *see* Thomas Jefferson

Dorothy Parker (1893–1967), American writer, poet and satirist. When in doubt one can always cite Dorothy Parker – and many do – for even if she didn't say it she might well have. Mrs Parker's fine but melancholy verse is wrongly overshadowed by her wit.

It's highly unlikely that Mrs Parker told a messenger, sent by an editor demanding her article: *'Tell him I've been too fucking busy – or vice versa.'* The remark is witty enough and Mrs Parker was never afraid to be bawdy, but it is also vulgar, which she was not. John Keats wrote in his definitive biography of Dorothy Parker.

> The anecdote sets her up as her own straight-man, and this was never her style. Her lines were invariably understated and murmured in a voice that further understated them. It would have been much

more in her style if she had heard some harassed writer snarl, 'Tell him I've been too fucking busy' and then for her to have muttered to herself, in accents of deepest sympathy for the poor, tired writer, 'Or vice versa.' That would have been much funnier.[337]

The real Parker style is captured by Arnold Gingrich, publisher of *Esquire*, who recalled: 'Once at a party I rather fatuously described myself as being just a simple country boy from Michigan – and heard a small voice murmur 'When convenient.'[338]

When the press magnate, William Randolph Hearst, built a bungalow at the MGM lot for his long-serving mistress, the actress Marion Davies, it had a madonna by the door. The following doggerel soon swept Hollywood . . .

> Upon my honor
> I saw a madonna
> Standing in a niche
> Above the door
> Of a prominent whore
> Of a prominent son of a bitch.[339]

. . . and was attributed to Mrs Parkewr, to her annoyance. She was a formidable counter-puncher, but never insulted anyone gratuitously. Besides, she would never have rhymed 'niche' with 'bitch'. (When Hearst died, Miss Davies was asked why she did not attend his funeral, as his wife and family did. 'I had him when he was alive. They can have him now he is dead.')

The story that *Clare Boothe Luce, about to go through a door at the same time as Mrs Parker, said 'Age before beauty', to which*

Mrs Parker replied 'Pearls before swine' and swept through triumphantly, is absurd. Mrs Luce would not have been that rude nor Mrs Parker so puerile. Indeed Mrs Luce was actually Mrs Brokaw on the only occasion the two met.[340]

Mrs Parker denied saying *'Everything worth doing is either immoral, illegal or fattening'*, which was one of Woollcott's, and: *'I'd rather flunk my Wassermann test/Than read the poems of Edgar Guest.'* A Wassermann test is for syphilis.[341] Edgar Guest wrote widely syndicated poems of saccharine morality and folksiness for the *Detroit Free Press*. Mr Woollcott (q.v.) said of Mrs Parker: 'So odd a blend of Little Nell and Lady Macbeth.'[342]

Calvin Coolidge (q.v.) was one of America's more phlegmatic presidents. When Mrs Parker was told Coolidge was dead, she was heard to wonder: *'How can they tell?'* As was fellow-wit Wilson Mizner, Alexander Woollcott (q.v.), *et al*. But that one may really be Mrs Parker's, as Robert Benchley is said to have answered straight back: 'He had an erection.' Benchley had a morbid fascination with death: funerary trade magazines littered his and Parker's office.[343] Erections in newly dead men are not uncommon.

Coventry Patmore (1823–96) was always an underrated poet and is now neglected as well. Two fine lines are no less fine for being pure wistful thinking . . .

> For mighty is the truth, it shall prevail
> When none cares whether it prevail or not

. . . although the first line should be: 'The truth is great, and shall prevail.' William Ernest Henley's *Invictus*, paraphrasing the Vulgate, has some equally magnificent untruths which don't detract from the poetry.

It matters not how straight the gate
How charged with punishment the scroll,
I am the master of my fate:
I am the captain of my soul.

Reading the poem one can, briefly, imagine its assertions are true.

St Paul, *see* the Bible

Hesketh Pearson, *see* Charles Lamb *and* Oscar Wilde

Samuel Pepys (1633–1703), English Admiralty official and diarist.

'*Tell it to the marines!*' Major William Drury of the Royal Marine Light Infantry put these words into the mouth of one of England's greatest diarists. Or at least into his ear. Drury claimed in 1904 that Charles II had told Pepys: '. . . ere we cast doubts upon a tale that lacketh likelihood, we will first tell it to the marines' (founded in 1664). Drury later recanted his story, or to be more precise, recast it as a fiction. Which was wise, since it is a piece of folk advice – Sir Walter Scott used it in *Redgauntlet* in 1824 and Lord Byron in *The Island* the year before – both predating Drury's version; and in vulgar, indeed coarser, form it predates Pepys's as well.[344] Marines were stationed on all Royal Navy ships to help maintain discipline and they were not liked by the sailors. The implication of the remark is 'The marines are so credulous they'll believe anything. Sailors aren't so silly.'

Needless to say, the Royal Marines have a different explanation. According to them, Pepys told His Majesty about flying fish. This sounded so unlikely that Charles asked a nearby officer of the Maritime Regiment of Foot if the tale were true, since: 'Only the marines with their wide-ranging service and experience could verify or negate any tall story.'[345] There is no contemporary verification for this tall story.

General John J. Pershing (1860–1948), Commander of the American Expeditionary Force in the Great War.

The Marquis de Lafayette enlisted in the American revolutionary army in 1777, and so forged a bond between France and America that has endured ever since. So when Pershing, stepping ashore in France at the head of the AEF, dedicated to preserving French freedom, cried: *'Lafayette, nous voilà'* ('Lafayette, we are here'), it carried deep historic and emotional overtones. This splendid cry was actually made by Lt.-Col. Charles E. Stanton (1859–1953) at the tomb of Lafayette in Paris on 4 July 1917 (American Independence Day) and repeated by him ten days later on Bastille Day (French independence day). Newspaper editors prefer even a boring quote from a 'big name' to an underling's useful comment. So to gain the best of both options it is common practice for the press to credit the quotes from juniors, like Stanton, to their seniors, like Pershing (who always gave Stanton the credit for the words).[346] For an earlier example *see* Henri IV.

(Henri) Phillippe Pétain, Marshal of France (1856–1951). The world likes the famous and infamous to be two-dimensional, the icons of unblemished purity, the villains of irredeemable villainy. Pétain causes problems. He was one of France's heroes in the Great War and one of her villains in the Second World War when he led the Vichy government (1940–45) which collaborated far too readily with Hitler.

Prior to Vichy, the marshal was best known for his noble phrase after taking command of the French defending forces at Verdun in 1916, *'Ils ne passeront pas'* – 'They shall not pass.' After the Second World War it was discovered that the author of those inspiring words was not the (now) ex-marshal but General Robert Nivelle (1856–1924) who included them in his Orders of the Day on 23 June that year. Correctly, *'Vous ne les laisserez pas passer'* – 'You shall not allow them to pass.' How convenient.[347]

Peter Pindar (pen-name of John Wolcot), *see* George M. Cohan

Philip II of Spain, *see* Christopher North

William Pitt, 1st Earl of Chatham ('Pitt the Elder', 1708–78), 'The Great Commoner': orator, statesman, champion of the American colonists and prime minister, 1756–61 and 1766–68.

When Pitt was a young MP the press were not 'the Fourth Estate, more important than them all'. Parliamentary reporters had to learn what had happened in the Commons through bribery and the versions given to them by MPs with their own partisan interests. There was an easier way, now hallowed by journalistic tradition: make it up. Thus it was with Pitt's great speech in early 1741 in reply to Sir Robert Walpole, the prime minister – a speech quoted by literate young men on the make.* *'The atrocious crime of being a young man ... I shall attempt neither to palliate nor deny, but content myself with wishing that I may be one of those whose follies may cease with their youth, and not one of that number who are ignorant in spite of experience.'* The speech was reported by Dr Samuel

* Old men who have made it prefer to quote 'Age is the begetting of wisdom.'

Johnson in *The Gentleman's Magazine* but, as he told his Boswell: 'That speech I wrote in a garret in Exeter Street.'[348] In 1738 the Commons asserted it was 'a notorious breach of privileges' for anyone to report the doings of the House. As late as 1771 the Lord Mayor of London was committed to the Tower for championing the right of printer–publishers to report the proceedings of Parliament.[349] *See also* Lord Acton.

William Pitt ('Pitt the Younger', 1759–1806), statesman, prime minister, 1783–1801 and 1804–6 who died in office from overwork and the alcohol that enabled him to do it.

Upon his return to the premiership in 1804, Pitt organized the alliance with Russia and Austria against France, but this was shattered by Bonaparte's great victory at Austerlitz two years later. Upon hearing the bad news Pitt died, saying: '*Alas my poor country*', or '*Oh my country, how I leave my country*', or '*How I love my country*', or '*My country, my country.*' All of these are too seemly, too politically useful and too numerous to carry the ring of truth. Oral tradition has Pitt saying: '*I think I could eat one of Bellamy's veal pies*', but another option seems the most probable. 'Another bottle of port, please.'[350]

Plato, *see* Sir Robert Armstrong

Alexander Pope (1688–1744), poet. Pope's use of English is so exact it is seldom possible to phrase his thoughts better.

It is, however, possible to phrase them worse, such as: '*A little knowledge is a dangerous thing*', but, as Edmund Burke (q.v.) said, 'There is no knowledge which is not valuable',[351] and Pope must be read in context . . .

A little learning is a dangerous thing,
Drink deep, or taste nor the Pierian Spring
There shallow draughts intoxicate the brain
And drinking largely sobers us again.[352]

... and knowledge is not the same thing as learning. The Pierides were the Muses, hence Pierian Spring.

To 'Damn with faint praise' is widely quoted but it lacks the pungent irony of the whole couplet – and it's always pleasing to score points by completing another person's incomplete quotation.

Damn with faint praise, assent with civil leer,
And without sneering, teach the rest to sneer.[353]

Pope also wrote 'The proper study of mankind is man',[354] but Aldous Huxley's variation is better: 'The proper study of mankind is books.'[355] *See also* the Bible *and* Robert Ingersoll

Colonel William Prescott (1726–95). American revolutionary soldier.

The first pitched battle in the American War of Independence didn't take place at Bunker Hill on 17 June 1775. Everyone concerned intended it should take place at Bunker Hill but the American commander, Colonel Prescott, fortified the nearby Breed's Hill by mistake, and there the battle took place. To simplify matters – or complicate them – Breed's Hill was, thereafter, often known as Bunker Hill.

Americans know it was at the battle of Breed's/Bunker Hill that the phrase '*Don't fire until you see the whites of their eyes*' was coined, some say, by Colonel Prescott; others say by General Israel Putnam. Some Germans know the remark was first used by King Frederick the Great in 1757; others know it was by Prince Charles of Prussia twelve years earlier.[356] One suspects Caveman Ug gave similar orders to his stone-clutching family as primeval carnivores approached their home.

Private Eye (1961–), British satirical fortnightly. The *Eye* has greatly enriched the English language with such phrases as 'Ugandan discussions' (sometimes 'East African') for enjoying, or at any rate having, sexual relations; 'Pass the sick-bag Alice' as a parody of John Junor, the self-righteous ex-editor of the *Sunday Express*; 'Confirmed bachelor' for homosexual and 'fun-loving' for promiscuous; 'So farewell then . . .' for E. J. Thribb, the resident poet and obituarist, and: 'Shome mishtake, surely?'.

However the *Eye* did not coin '*Who he? Ed.*' Harold Ross, the legendary editor of *The New Yorker*, would write this on the edge of galley proofs along with equally terse comments such as 'What mean?'[357] Nor did the *Eye* coin '*Small but perfectly formed*', which was most often applied to the long-time, long-suffering editor of the *Observer*, Donald Trelford. The phrase was used by Duff Cooper (1st Viscount Norwich) writing to his future wife, then Lady Diana Manners: 'I really did enjoy Belvoir you know . . . You must, I think, have enjoyed it too with your two stout lovers frowning at one another across the hearthrug, while your small but perfectly formed one kept the party in a roar.'[358]

Aurelius Propertius, *see* Andrew Jackson

Pierre Joseph Proudhon, *see* Karl Marx

Marcel Proust (1871–1922), author of the part-work novel *Remembrance of Things Past* (*A la Recherche du Temps Perdu*).

The delicious telegram rejecting an invitation, '*Impossible to come. Lie follows*', appears in volume 1, chapter 1, but three years earlier Ralph Nevill wrote of Lord Charles Beresford: 'When at the eleventh hour he had been summoned to dine with the then Prince of Wales, he is said to have telegraphed back: 'Very sorry, can't come. Lie follows by post.' This story has been told of several other people, but Lord Charles was the real originator.'[359]

Proverbial '*The exception proves the rule.*' Only fools parrot this nonsense, but it is depressing how many fools there are. The phrase comes from the Latin tag '*Exceptio probat regulum*', which does indeed mean 'The exception proves the rule', but 'prove' is used in the sense of testing, as in proving a gun-barrel. The correct translation of the tag into demotic English is: 'The exception tests the rule.' In full the Latin is: '*Exceptio probat regulum in casibus exceptis.*'[360] Robert Burton in his *Anatomy of Melancholy* took the more sophisticated and arguable view: 'No rule is so general, which admits not some exception.' *See also* The Golden Rule *and* William Shakespeare

Publishers' Publicists, *see* Val Hennessy

Israel Putnam, *see* Colonel William Prescott

Q

Francis Quarles (1592–1644), poet and Chronologer to the City of London, whose wife bore him eighteen children.

Mr Quarles's original, uncontentious assertion was not '*You can only die once*', but: 'It is the lot of man to die but once.'[361] Whether this was said to encourage or discourage those on this mortal coil is not clear. Quarles's books and manuscripts were burned by the Puritans – which is all you need to know to be a royalist.

Thomas Danforth Quayle (1947–), vice-president of the United States of America, 1988–92, is no clear-thinking, silver-tongued orator. Nor is he the certifiable idiot portrayed by those proponents of objective journalism, the American press corps.

On a trip to Latin America, Vice-President Quayle's remark '*I wish I'd studied Latin at school so I could talk to you in your own language*' was too good to ignore – even after Democratic Congresswoman Pat Schroeder publicly apologized to Mr Quayle for inventing it. The remark lives on in popular folk myth as the genuine article.

A genuine Quaylism is: 'We offer the Party as a big tent. How we do that within the platform, the preamble to the platform or whatnot remains to be seen. But that message will have to be articulated with great clarity.'[362] This has not yet been decoded.

R

Allan Ramsay, *see* Sir Walter Scott

Rudolf Eric Raspe, *see* Baron von Munchausen

James Ray, *see* Samuel Butler (the earlier)

Johnnie Ray (1927–90) was variously known as the Prince of Wails, the Nabob of Sob and the Howling Success.

In 1957 Ray's song, *Yes, Tonight Josephine*, reached number one in the charts and British wags began using '*Not tonight Josephine*' as a way of saying 'No' in a witty and amusing fashion (or not, according to taste). Parents of bobby-soxers worried about Ray's overtly sexual stage performances. This was unnecessary. Ray was not interested in Josephines, nor anyone of the opposite sex.

This cliché has nothing to do with (Marie) Josèphine-Rose Tascher de la Pagerie (1763–1814), sometime Vicomtesse de Beauharnais, later Empress of France. It has less than nothing to do with her last husband, Napoleon Bonaparte.

George Robey's earlier use of the phrase has been forgotten by everyone.

Ronald Wilson Reagan (1911–), actor and after-dinner speaker, President of the Screen Actors' Guild, 1947–52, and the United States of America, 1981–9. Gore Vidal described him at the time of his election to the White House as 'a triumph of the embalmer's art'.[363] Ronald Wilson Reagan arrived from Hollywood where he learned to expect his scripts well in advance and all performances to be properly produced, directed and stage-managed. Never has an administration been more orchestrated and the American media more manipulated than during the Reagan 'revolution'.

Reagan's press secretary was Larry Speakes, who revealed in his biography, *Speaking Out*, not only that he coined many of the president's more uplifting soundbites but that he didn't bother the president with them beforehand. One was to celebrate the Reagan–Gorbachev summit in Geneva in 1985: '*There is much that divides us, but I believe the world breathes easier because we are here talking together.*' The hilarious end to this story was the synthetic outrage with which the press and former presidential press secretaries greeted these 'revelations' with such headlines as 'UnSpeakable' in the *Washington Post*. Mr Speakes was forced to resign his overpaid job as spokesperson for Merrill Lynch, America's largest stockbrokers, for the sin of 'showing the audience how the scenery moved'.

Such attitudes worked both ways. Reagan habitually credited his political opponents with any comments he thought they said, or which they might have said, or which it would have been convenient to him if they had said. One example of many is his quoting Harold Ickes (1874–1952), Franklin Roosevelt's Secretary of the Interior, as saying: '*What we were striving for was a kind of modified form of communism.*' There is no record of Ickes ever saying or writing anything remotely akin to those words. Less controversially, Reagan was fond of quoting Winston Churchill's dictum: '*The idea that a nation can tax itself into prosperity is one of the crudest delusions that has ever befuddled the human mind*', marred only by the inability of Churchill scholars to find any such words by Churchill. But then the Great Communicator was concerned with the theatrical integrity of his performances, not their veracity. Voltaire took the Reaganesque view: 'It is necessary always to aim at being interesting rather than exact, for the spectator forgives everything except boredom.' ('*Il faut toujours songer à être intéressant plutôt qu'exact car le spectateur pardonne tout, sauf La langueur.*'[364] An entire book has been devoted to such 'lapses' by Reagan.[365]

William Lutz recounts the Republican commercial, in Reagan's 1984 re-election campaign, which claimed that their Ronnie had given federal workers cost-of-living pay increases '. . . in spite of those who tried to stop him doing what we elected him to do'. Actually not. Such increases had been required by law since 1975 and Reagan thrice tried to eliminate them. When taxed with this seeming discrepancy, a Republican official asked, seriously, 'Since when is a commercial supposed to be accurate?'[366]

Many of Reagan's best remarks were lifted straight from films and the anecdotage of show business. He displayed great courage in remarking to his wife after being shot: '*Honey, I forgot to duck*', but the line is Jack Dempsey's to his wife after he lost the world heavyweight championship to Gene Tunney on 23 September 1926.[367] *See also* Henry Kissinger, Thomas Jefferson *and* Knute Rockne.

John Reed, *see* Lincoln Steffens

Lord Reith (Sir John Reith, 1889–1971), managing director of the British Broadcasting Company Ltd. in 1926. Reith became first Director-General of the British Broadcasting Corporation in 1927, at £6,000 a year, for his unqualified support for the government during the General Strike.

Reith, a stern Scots Presbyterian, stamped his puritanism firmly on the BBC. '*Nation shall speak peace unto nation*' is the splendid biblical motto he gave the Corporation. It is actually an adaptation from the book of Micah, 'Nation shall not lift up sword against nation.'[368] The adaptation was not, as automatically assumed, by Reith, but by Dr Montague Rendall, classics scholar, headmaster of Winchester and vice-president, 1927–33, of the BBC.

Dr Montague Rendall, *see* Lord Reith

Miss Mandy Rice-Davies, *see under* Viscount Astor

Céser Ritz (1850–1918) hotelier. The Savoy Hotel boasts of having employed both Ritz as its manager and the great Auguste Escoffier as head chef; it remains coy about sacking them both for fiddling the books. One of Ritz's maxims, *'the customer is always right'*, has become traditional but he expressed it differently. *'Le client n'a jamais tort'* – 'The customer is never wrong.'[369] It just depends which side of the counter you're on.

Marquis de La Rochejaquelein, *see* Benito Mussolini

Knute K. Rockne (1888–1931) was the fabled football coach for Notre Dame University with a nice line in inspirational aphorisms. He is credited with *'When the going gets tough, the tough get going.'* So is Joseph P. Kennedy.[370]

One of Rockne's star players was George Gipp (1895–1920) who, dying of pneumonia on 14 December 1920, said: *'One day, when the going is tough and a big game is hanging in the balance, ask the team to win one for the Gipper. I don't know where I'll be, Rock, but I'll know about it and I'll be happy'* and passed away. Eight years later on 12 November 1928, when 'the Fighting Irish' were in a bad way with the half-time score 0–0, Rockne finally told the story and begged his team to 'Win one for the Gipper' and they did, 12–6. Ronald Reagan played George Gipp in the 1941 film *Knute Rockne, All American*: it was one of his favourite roles and he would quote the Gipper's last words on the slightest provocation, or none. Those words were not the Gipper's but made up by Rockne, who would never have let a story like that lie fallow for eight years if he had thought of it sooner. Indeed, he had used that same story to inspire several earlier Notre Dame teams.[371] *See also* Leo Durocher.

Will Rogers (1879–1935), American comedian and homespun philosopher. Rogers was widely liked and liked widely but he was neither foolish enough nor dishonest enough to say '*I never met a man I didn't like*', as reported by the *Saturday Evening Post*.[372] What he said was: 'I joked about every prominent man in my lifetime, but I never met one I didn't like.' He is one of the many people who did not originate '*Everybody talks about the weather but nobody does anything about it*', for which *see* Mark Twain. *See also* Capitalists.

President Franklin D. Roosevelt (1888–1945), thirty-second and longest-serving president of the United States, 1933–45.

The Daughters of the American Revolution (all claiming descent from soldiers and patriots of 1776) would deny they are a snobbish group which looks down on more recent arrivals – but nobody else would. It therefore gave many Americans much harmless pleasure when 'F. D. R.' began a speech to a DAR convention '*Fellow immigrants*',[373] or at least it would have done had he said it. He did express similar sentiments but, as usual, it was an attendant journalist who stripped the president's views down to less than their core.

On 7 April 1932 in one of his radio 'Fireside Chats' to the nation, the president said: 'These unhappy times call for the building of plans that ... put their faith once more in *the forgotten man at the bottom of the economic pyramid*', and 'the forgotten man' entered the political lexicon. Roosevelt borrowed the phrase from Professor William Graham Sumner of Yale, but who remembers him?[374]

In the Congressional Record for 22 September 1950 you can find Roosevelt saying: '... *there is nothing wrong with the Communists in this country; several of the best friends I have got are Communists.*' The story behind those words tells us more about the Congress than about Roosevelt. Representative Harold Velde inserted into the Record an article written by one-time Representative Martin Dies that claimed Roosevelt made the remark to him in 1938. The validity of the claim can be judged by the fact that Dies said he had put the conversation into his 1940 book *The Trojan Horse in America* – but it ain't there.[375]

No other major democracy allows its parliamentarians to insert whatever they please into the record of their proceedings. Thus, in 1820, Congressman Felix Walker from North Carolina was reading a parochial speech which his fellow legislators started barracking. Walker waved them aside: 'I am not talking for your ears, I am only talking for Buncombe', the main town in his district. Thus he gave us the word 'bunk' or 'bunkum'. Walker still lost his seat at the next election. The back-formation, 'debunk', did not appear for another century. *See also* Winston L. S. Churchill, Charles de Gaulle, Alice Roosevelt Longworth *and* General Douglas MacArthur.

President Roosevelt, 'although nobody's sure which one', *see* George M. Cohan.

President Theodore Roosevelt (1858–1919), cowboy, big-game hunter and twenty-sixth president of the United States, 1901–09.

Every patriotic American knows two things about this jingoistic president: that the 'Teddy bear' was named after he refused to shoot a bear cub while on a hunting trip near the Little Sunflower River in Mississippi and that he described his foreign policy as '*Walk softly and carry a big stick.*' So he did, but he didn't invent the idea, telling a Minnesota crowd: 'There is a homely adage which runs: "Walk softly and carry a bit stick – you will go far."'[376] *See also* his daughter, Alice Roosevelt Longworth.

Sir Francis Rose, *see* Gertrude Stein

Harold Ross of *The New Yorker, see Private Eye*

Thomas Rowley was a fifteenth-century monk whose poetry, discovered in the eighteenth century, was highly regarded with editions of his works published in 1778 and 1882. He is now forgotten – unlike Thomas Chatterton (1752–70) who attributed his poems to the fictitious Rowley and then committed suicide at seventeen.

Leo Rosten, *see* W. C. Fields

Jean-Jacques Rousseau, *see* Marie-Antoinette

R. W. 'Tiny' Rowland, *see* Edward Heath

Damon Runyon, *see* Napoleon Bonaparte *and* Frank Ward O'Malley

Bertrand Russell, 3rd Earl Russell (1872–1970), philosopher, philanderer and pacifist.

At the height of the cold war the principal weapon was rhetoric, hence the Right's improbable rallying cry, 'Better dead than Red'. The well-meaning Left riposted with *'Better Red than dead'*, which Alexander Solzhenitsyn accredited to the pacifist leader, Bertrand Russell – but it is such an obvious reply it seems to have arisen by spontaneous generation.[377] A. E. Housman observed drily of Russell: 'If I were the Prince of Peace I would choose a less provocative ambassador.'[378] *See also* Lincoln Steffens.

S

Rafael Sabatini, *see* Yale University

William Safire, *see* Spiro Agnew *and* Woodrow Wilson

Robert Cecil, 3rd Marquess of Salisbury, *see* R. A. Butler *and* Francis I

Robert Cecil, 5th Marquess of Salisbury (1893–1972), landed aristocrat and politician.

Only in Britain would Lord Salisbury's comment on Iain Macleod, *'He is too clever by half'*, be a jibe. In France, for example, it would undoubtedly have been seen as a compliment. At the time Macleod was Colonial Secretary, busy giving independence to the Colonies in line with Harold Macmillan's 'winds of change' policy (q.v.), to which Salisbury was opposed. Salisbury did not call Macleod too clever by half but said: 'He is, as we all know, a man of most unusual intellectual brilliance; and he is, moreover, both brave and resolute. Those are valuable and not too common attributes in politics. But the fact remains that he has adopted especially in his relationship to the white community in Africa, a most unhappy and entirely wrong approach. He has been too clever by half.'[379] The generalized apophthegm from Salisbury's specific criticism seriously damaged Macleod's standing in the minds of the voting public.

(Henry) 'Red' Sanders, *see* Leo Durocher

Andrew Sarris, *see* Spencer Tracy

Joseph M. Schenck, *see* Samuel Goldwyn

C. P. Scott (1846–1932), was the great editor of the *Manchester Guardian* for fifty-seven years until 1929. Scott may, or may not, have said of the exciting new medium *'Television! No good will come of this device. The word is half Latin and half Greek'*,[380] but if he did he was in good company. The joke seems to have occurred to all the eminent classicists of the time – and to have been claimed by all the others.

George C. Scott, *see* Tom Berenger

Sir Walter Scott Bt. (1771–1832), appropriately named Scots poet and novelist.

Scots know that their national novelist coined *'Blood is thicker than water'* which occurs in *Guy Mannering* (1815). Americans know that the words were coined by Commodore

Josiah Tattnall in 1860, to justify his assisting a British naval squadron off the China coast. Tattnall was born near Savannah but was educated in England. The impartial scholar knows that the phrase appeared in Allan Ramsay's *Collection Of Scottish Proverbs* of 1737 and was old then.[381] Euripides's Andromache who used the phrase in 426 BC may not have been the first to do so. Blood has a specific gravity of 1.06; it is thicker than water with a specific gravity of 1.00. *See also* Baron von Munchhausen *and* Samuel Pepys.

Robert Service, *see* Charles Darwin

La Marquise de Sévigné (1626–96) is credited with '*No man is a hero to his valet*' or: '*Il n'y a point de héros pour son valet de chambre*', but she was only quoting the remark of Mme Anne-Marie Corneul (1605–94).[382] The put-down became so well known that Lord Byron could write satirically: 'In short he was a perfect cavallero, and to his very valet seemed a hero.'[383] If no man is a hero to his valet, what man can be a hero to his wife?

William Shakespeare (1564–1616). The immortal Bard, the Swan of Avon, the Wonder of his Age *et cetera*.

Some of Shakespeare's greatest lines are not by him (nor even by Francis Bacon, the Earl of Oxford, Ben Jonson or who ever else might have written his plays and sonnets). Both '*Off with his head, so much for Buckingham*', and '*A horse, a horse. My kingdom for a horse*' in *King Richard III* (Acts IV and V) were interpolated by Colley Cibber — actor, playwright and Poet Laureate — when producing those plays.[384]

'*Alas!, poor Yorick. I knew him well!*' is not even a good précis. Yorick had been dead twenty-three years and Hamlet, speaking, was then thirty-four. What Hamlet says is 'Alas!

poor Yorick. I knew him Horatio; a fellow of infinite jest and excellent fancy; he hath borne me on his back a thousand times; and now, how abhorred in my imagination it is! my gorge rises at it. Here hung those lips that I have kissed I know not how oft. Where be your gibes now? your gambols? your songs? your flashes of merriment, that were wont to set the table in a roar?'[385]

'*There's method in his madness*' is a useful notion, but not what Polonius said of Hamlet in one of those Asides heard by everyone except the person nearest him. 'Though this be madness, yet there is method in't.'[386] One day you may be in a conversation where a method actor is mentioned: do not miss the once-in-a-lifetime opportunity to say, deadpan, 'Ah, but there's madness in his method.'

''*Twas caviar to the general*' always puzzled me when young. Why not 'Caviar to the admiral'? Was this because the sturgeon is a freshwater fish? Put into context the words makes sense. Hamlet, addressing the players at Elsinore, recalls an earlier drama: 'The play, I remember, pleased not the million, 'twas caviar to the general',[387] that is, to the general public – it was an acquired taste, which few acquired. The air-bladder of the sturgeon was used to make isinglass.

'*All that glitters is not gold*' is usually attributed to Shakespeare, even though in *The Merchant of Venice* the Prince of Morocco, upon opening the golden casket and receiving a nasty surprise, actually exclaims: 'All that glisters is not gold.'[388] The warning is as old as cupidity and as modern as sin. The Bard was followed by Edmund Spenser in *Faerie Queene* (1589), Thomas Middleton in *A Fair Quarrel* (1617), John Dryden in *The Hind And The Panther* (1687) and Thomas Gray in *Ode On The Death of A Favourite Cat* (1747) and David Garrick in his prologue to *She Stoops to Conquer* in 1773. They may have been inspired by Shakespeare but

Barnabe Googe* in his *Eglogs, Epytaphs & Sonnetes* (1563) was not. Neither was *Heywood's Proverbs* (1546)[389] nor Geoffrey Chaucer, 'But all thing which that shineth as the gold, Ne is no gold, as I have heard it told' (*c.* 1387) in *The Canon's Yeoman's Tale*. According to Tyrwhitt,[390] Chaucer himself took the line from *Paraboloe* by Alanus de Insulis (d. 1294). '*Non teneas aurum totum quod splendet et aurum.*' Across the Channel at about the same time Denise Cordelier (*c.* 1300) had the same thought in *Le Diz de Freire*. '*Que tout n'est pars ors c'on voit loire.*'[391] This quotation should be reassigned to the entry Proverbial.

Anyone who has attempted '*To gild the lily*' knows it is a silly phrase. Shakespeare was never silly and his lines make sense:

> To gild refined gold, to paint the lily
> To throw a perfume on a violet
> To smooth the ice, or add another hue
> Unto the rainbow[392]

Gold has always had a fascination for mankind which goes beyond its function as money, as a secure store of value.

The Bard said 'The better part of valour is discretion',[393] but the general public turned this round to the neater '*Discretion is the better part of valour.*'

Shakespeare did write in *Hamlet, Prince of Denmark*:

> But to my mind, though I am native here
> And to the manner born – it is a custom
> More honoured in the breech than the observance

* 'A member of both universities' as *The Oxford Companion to English Literature* (1933 ed. p. 327) neatly tells us.

To the manor born is a useful but different phrase, authored by Anon. You can be to the manner born in Skid Row but if to the manor born you should never learn what Skid Row is. *See also* John Maynard Keynes. For Shakespeare, *see also* Francis Bacon, the Bible, Theodore Dreiser, Joseph Heller *and* Ben Jonson.

Bill Shankly, *see* Leo Durocher

William Shatner, *see* Captain James T. Kirk

(George) Bernard Shaw (1856–1950), music critic, dramatist, self-publicist.

Sam Goldwyn (q.v.) realized that great movies require great scripts, which meant great writers, but he never managed to grasp the Inevitable next step — that great writers cost great money. So when Goldwyn was negotiating to buy the film rights to Shaw's plays, he emphasized the artistic integrity of his productions while Shaw emphasized the money. The talks failed, and the playwright's fabled comment to the tycoon explained why: '*The trouble, Mr Goldwyn, is that you are only interested in art and I am only intereted in money.*' It was Goldwyn's head of publicity, Howard Dietz, who invented the famous witticism which so delighted Shaw that he never repudiated its authorship.[394]

In *The Doctor's Dilemma* (1911, Act III) Shaw writes: '*All professions are conspiracies against the laity*', but he is summarizing Adam Smith. 'People of the same trade seldom meet together, even for merriment and diversion, but the conversation ends in a conspiracy against the public, or in some contrivance to raise prices.'[395] In that context there is no difference between the Law Society and the National Union of Mineworkers.

There is an oft-told tale of a lady saying to Shaw: 'You have the greatest brain in the world and I have the most beautiful body; so we ought to produce the most perfect child', to which Shaw riposted: 'What if the child inherits my body and your brains?' The lady has been named as Jean Harlow, Mary Pickford, Elinor Glynn or Mrs Patrick Campbell, and even Marilyn Monroe. The story is untrue when applied to any female icon. The lady, who wrote to Shaw from Zurich, remains unnamed.[396] *See also* Humphrey Bogart.

Sir Hartley Shawcross (Lord Shawcross of Friston, 1903–), British lawyer and middle-of-the-road politician.

Winston Churchill said in 1950, after the Labour government had lost most of its huge 1945 majority in the general election that year: 'No one will be able to boast *"We are the masters now"*', and the last part of that phrase ensured notoriety for Shawcross, who hadn't said it and clearly hadn't meant anything like it either. On 2 April 1946 Shawcross was speaking for the newly victorious government in the Commons and quoted Lewis Carroll's *Alice in Wonderland*. '"But" said Alice, "the question is whether you can make a word mean different things." "Not so," said Humpty Dumpty, "the question is which is to be the master. That's all."' Shawcross added: 'We are the masters of the moment, and not only of the moment but for a very long time to come.' Shawcross was a right-wing member of the Labour Party but, just as easily, could have been a left-wing member of the Conservative Party.

Philip Sheridan (1831–88), a West Point graduate, and later an American general, credited with never having lost a battle.

When the Comanche warrior Toch-a-way was presented to Sheridan in 1869 he said: 'Me good Indian', and the general's unfortunate observation was that *the only good Indian is a dead Indian*', which has been applied to various besieged minorities (and majorities) ever since. The story is vouchsafed to us by Edward M. Ellis who claims he was present at Old Fort Cobb when that diplomatic exchange took place. Sheridan later denied the remark but took no issue with the sentiment, having applied his considerable military abilities in helping to obliterate what was left of the Indian nations after the Civil War.[397]

Richard Brinsley Sheridan (1751–1816), playwright, wit and politician.

Of all Sheridan's *bons mots* the best is, I suggest, his riposte to Robert Dundas: '*The Right Hon. gentleman is indebted to his memory for his jests and his imagination for his facts.*'[398] Sheridan was lucky in his biographer, the poet Thomas Moore, who sculpted that version from Sheridan's less deft original. 'The Right Hon. gentleman has drawn upon his memory for his eloquence and upon his imagination for his facts.'[399] Possibly Sheridan had read *Gil Blas* (1715): 'One may say his wit sparkles at the expense of his memory.' ('*On peut dire que son esprit brille aux dépens de sa mémoire.*')[400]

The form is an old one. Harold Macmillan said: 'As usual the Liberals offer a mixture of sound and original ideas. Unfortunately none of the sound ideas is original and none of the original ideas is sound',[401] but it was not Sheridan he was paraphrasing but Dr Johnson. 'Sir, your manuscript is both good and original; but the part that is good is not original and the part that is original is not good.'

William Tecumseh Sherman (1820–91), American general.

The great villain of *Gone With the Wind*, General Sherman exacted some of the most thorough damage to the Confederacy by Union forces.

In a speech in Columbus, Ohio in August 1880, Sherman declared: 'There is many a boy here today who looks on war as all glory, but, boys, it is all hell', which reappeared in newspaper accounts as '*War is Hell.*'[402]

In retirement Sherman was urged by General Henderson to seek the Republican nomination for the 1884 presidential election. His pleasing response was a legendary telegram: '*If asked I will not stand. If drafted I will not run. If elected I will not serve.*' The story would have been perfect if Sherman had then been drafted and elected, but his actual telegram, witty enough, ended the matter. 'I will not accept if nominated and will not serve if elected.'[403]

(Richard) 'Red' Skelton, *see* Samuel Goldwyn

Adam Smith, *see* Napoleon *and* George Bernard Shaw

John L. B. Soule, *see* Horace Greeley

Robert Southey, *see* Edward Bulwer Lytton

Larry Speakes, *see* Ronald W. Reagan

Mr Spock, *see* Captain James T. Kirk

Countess Spencer, currently La Comtesse de Chambrun, formerly Miss Raine McCorquodale, Mrs Gerald Legge, Viscountess Lewisham, Countess of Dartmouth and Countess Spencer, *see* Charles Prince of Wales

Edmund Spenser, *see* William Shakespeare

Herbert Spencer (1820–1903), pioneer of evolutionary philosophy.

Spencer was in the Athenaeum one day when he heard an eminent judge, Charles Roupell, remark: '*To play billiards well is the sign of a misspent youth.*' Spencer repeated the aphorism and, to his annoyance, it was assummed to be by him. He should have been grateful it was not assumed to be about him.[404] *See also* Charles Darwin.

Revd Dr William A. Spooner (1844–1930), Dean and then Warden of New College, Oxford from 1876 to 1924. Dr Spooner suffered from the form of metathesis – now known as Spoonerism – where pairs of initial letters, syllables or words are transposed.

Once in chapel he announced the hymn to be sung as 'Kinquering Kongs their Titles Take', and on another occasion led prayers with: 'Darken our lightness, we beseech Thee O Lord', and advised his flock that 'the Lord is a shoving leopard.' Those are authenticated Spoonerisms, but once the habit became known every Oxford wag devoted himself to composing new ones. The reprimand to an undergraduate: '*You have tasted two worms, you have hissed my mystery lectures and you must leave by the first town drain*' is certainly spurious, as is '*Mardon me Padom, this pile is occupewed, allow me to sew you to another sheet*', and, during the Great War: '*When the boys come home from France we'll have the hags flung out.*' Those are too lovingly crafted to have arisen from metathesis, or even serendipity. The toast to '*Our queer old Dean*' is as improbable as '*sporn-rimmed hectacles*', '*a scoop of boy trouts*' and a '*well-boiled icicle*'.[405]

Spooner was unaware of those little slips. As far as he was concerned they were all lace Bibles.[406]

Lt.-Col. Charles E. Stanton, *see* General John J. Pershing

Lincoln Steffens (1866–1936), American populist journalist.

Steffens is credited with: '*I have seen the future and it works*', the paradigm of all those well-meaning *ingénues* who went to Communist Russia between the Wars, saw the show-sites of happy, healthy proletarian workers and returned home marvelling. Steffens was part of an American team visiting Russia in 1919, and upon his returned exclaimed: 'I have been over into the future, and it works.' The press, as so often, pared down Steffens's aphorism to the punchier form – which the author then adopted.

Another American journalist credited with the remark is John Reed, who in 1919 published *Ten Days That Shook The World*, a book sympathetic to the new Russian regime. In 1974 the writer Philip Toynbee visited America and wrote: 'I have seen the future and it doesn't work' – but it works a lot better than Russian Communism ever did.[407]

The English – as reluctant to attribute quotations to Americans as Americans are to attribute them to Englishmen* – have given the credit for 'I have seen the future and it works' to Sidney and Beatrice Webb, the upper-class socialist intellectuals. Mrs Webb said of herself when young: '*If I ever felt inclined to be timid as I was going into a room full of people I would say to myself: "You're the cleverest member of one of the cleverest families in the cleverest class of the cleverest nation in the world. Why should you be frightened?"*' As we have only

---

* See the entries for Sir Noel Coward and Spencer Tracy.

hearsay evidence of this remark, from the philosopher Bertrand Russell, it too is probably apocryphal.[408]

Gertrude Stein (1874–1946), American author and self-confessed genius. The Jeanette Winterson of her day.

In 1931, Edmund Wilson wrote of Gertrude Stein: 'With sentences so regularly rhythmical, so needlessly prolix, so many times repeated and ending so often in present participles, the reader is all too soon in a state ... to fall asleep.'[409] If the selfsame reader had a gun pressed to his head and was asked for a Gertrude Stein quote, he might respond with great surety: '*A rose is a rose is a rose*', and then be summarily shot. In her poem *Sacred Emily*[410] Miss Stein, a woman of maximum output and minimal vocabulary, writes of the English painter Sir Francis Rose Bt., 'Rose is a rose is a rose', commenting on the rosiness of Rose rather than the rosiness of a rose. The rosiness is unremarkable as Sir Francis, then Master Rose, was only three years old at the time.

According to Jack Freedman, 'A piano is a piano is a piano' was written by Gertrude Steinway.

Ms Stein is also credited with the phrase '*A lost generation*', but this, she always admitted, came from a Monsieur Pernollet, a hotelier from Belley, who referred to a mechanic fixing Ms Stein's car as one of '*Une génération perdue*'; those whose formative years had been spent at war. Ms Stein applied the phrase to Ernest Hemingway and his circle and Hemingway quoted her in *The Sun Also Rises* (1926).[411]

What annoys authors most about publishers' rejection slips is their standardized nature. At least Ms Stein could not complain about that when A. J. Fifield sent her a rejection slip in her own all too imitable style.

I am only one, only one, only. Only one being, one at the same time. Not two, not three, only one. Only one life to live, only sixty minutes in one hour. Only one pair of eyes. Only one brain. Only one being. Being only one, having only one pair of eyes, having only one time, having only one life. I cannot read your ms three or four times. Not even one time. Only one look, only one look is enough. Hardly one copy would sell here. Hardly one. Hardly one.[412]

Rejection slips from Frank Crowninshield, the great editor of *Vanity Fair*, had to be read twice. He once sent a manuscript back to Paul Gallico with the note: 'My Dear Boy, This is superb! A little masterpiece! What colour! What life! How beautifully you have phrased it all! A veritable gem! Why don't you take it round to *Harper's Bazaar*?'[413]

John Steinbeck, *see* John Wayne

Mrs Harriet Beecher Stowe (1811–96), appears on the title page of *Uncle Tom's Cabin* as the author of the book, although she modestly admitted she never wrote it. 'God wrote it. I merely wrote to his dictation.' In its day the book infuriated slave-owners – Uncle Tom is flogged to death by Simon Legree for refusing to divulge the hiding-place of two runaway slaves – but today it infuriates African–Americans who are outraged at Uncle Tom's lack of late twentieth-century political correctness.

Although Mrs Stowe credited the Almighty with writing *Uncle Tom's Cabin*, she credited herself with the royalties.

Maximilien de Béthune, duc de Sully, *see* Henri IV

Billy Sunday, *see* Robert G. Ingersoll

Willie Sutton (1901–80), American safe-cracker.

Willie 'The Actor' Sutton was a thief for all seasons, a man who raised breaking and entering to an art form. A master of disguise with million-dollar fingertips, Sutton had a string of 'successes' in the thirties until he was apprehended and convicted. Despite the occasional jail break, he spent the rest of his career behind bars, no doubt the pride of that particular penitentiary. His best-known quote, '*I rob banks because that's where the money is*', was actually put into his mouth by a reporter. In *I, Willie Sutton* (1953), he confessed that 'It is a rather pleasant experience to be alone in a bank at night', a remark more in keeping with a man of his sophistication and sensitivity.[414]

Dean (Jonathan) Swift, *see* Thomas Babington Macaulay

Herbert Bayard Swope, *see* Bernard Baruch

T

Stephen G. Tallentyre (pen-name of E. Beatrice Hall), *see* Voltaire

'Talleyrand', Charles Maurice de Talleyrand-Périgord, Prince de Benevento (1754–1838).

All the reference books point out that Talleyrand is generally credited with the opinion: '*It is worse than a crime. It is a blunder*' on the execution of the duc d'Enghien by

Bonaparte on 21 March 1804. Most of them add that this remark should be attributed to Joseph Fouché (1763–1820), who claimed it in his *Mémoires*. Some point out that it should, more correctly, be: 'It is more than a crime. It is a political mistake' (or 'political fault' depending on how you translate it). None I have seen add that it probably doesn't belong to Fouché either, as his sons claimed the *Mémoires* were spurious.[415] Benham adds Boulay de la Meurthe to the list of possible authors.[416] The original is less deft than the pastiche, but more interesting. Crimes and blunders can usually be made good, but political mistakes can seldom be rectified, making them a far more heinous offence. *See also* John Dryden.

Tarzan, Lord Greystoke, *see* Edgar Rice Burroughs

Bishop Jeremy Taylor, *see* Thomas Babington Macaulay

Norman Tebbit (Lord Tebbit, 1931–), British Cabinet minister, was said to have callously advised job-hunters: *'Get on yer bike.'*

'The origin of my much misquoted and misrepresented phrase', Lord Tebbit told me, 'lay in the speech I delivered, as Secretary of State for Employment, replying to a debate on unemployment at the Conservative Party's annual conference in Blackpool in October 1981. The concern at the time was the trend towards the unemployed in certain areas rioting as the unemployment figures increased. I said: ". . . I know these problems. I grew up in the thirties with an unemployed father. He didn't riot, he got on his bike and looked for work and he kept looking until he found it." The speech was very well received by the conference but I have been correcting its misuse ever since.'[417]

Alfred, Lord Tennyson (1809–92), poet. The Laureate's great lament for his youthful love Arthur Hallam, *In Memoriam* (1850), was written by Queen Victoria. See the conclusive proofs set out by Monseigneur Ronald Knox – using the same systems by which the Baconians 'prove' Francis Bacon (q.v.) wrote the plays of Shakespeare.[418] *See also* Lincoln Steffens.

Margaret Thatcher (Baroness Thatcher, 1925–), British prime minister 1979–90.

While possessing many unique political talents, Margaret Thatcher was denied the gift of memorable phrasemaking, and her English is utilitarian. Her quotable remarks only achieve their status from her status. 'I am extraordinarily patient, provided I get my own way in the end', would not be noteworthy from the chairwoman of the Grantham Women's Institute. Her only great phrase '*You turn if you want. The Lady's not for turning*', was written for her by the playwright Sir Ronald Millar. 'It puns on Christopher Fry's play *The Lady's Not For Burning* (1948) set in the year 1400. The lady in question, Jennet Jordemayne, is accused of turning the local rag-and-bone man into a dog.'[419] Some say Lady Thatcher achieved a similar metamorphosis with her ministers.

Bishop Theodoret of Cyrrhus, *see* Julian called 'The Apostate'

Jacques-Anatole-François Thibault, *see* Anatole France

Henry David Thoreau, *see* Thomas Jefferson

James Thurber, *see* Samuel Goldwyn

Tiberius (Tiberus Claudius Nero) Emperor of Rome, *see*
The Bible

Philip Toynbee, *see* Lincoln Steffens

Spencer Tracy (1900–67), American actor. When asked
the secret of acting Mr Tracy replied: *'Know your lines, speak
up and don't bump into the furniture'*, but this is a traditional
actors' joke. *See also* Sir Noel Coward.

Tracy and Katherine Hepburn, destined to be the great
loves of each others' lives, met for the first time in 1942
ahead of *The Woman of the Year* in which they were to co-
star. Hepburn said: *'I'm afraid I'm a little tall for you Mr
Tracy'* to which filmland tradition says he replied: 'Don't
worry. I'll soon cut you down to size.' Filmland tradition is
a lying jade. The response was from Miss Hepburn's escort,
Joseph L. Mankiewicz,[420] of whom Andrew Sarris said 'His
wit scratches more than it bites.'[421]

Traditional In July 1962, when the Attorney-General, Sir
Reginald Manningham-Buller Bt. QC MP (known as Bully-
ing-Manner from his courtroom methods) was promoted to
Lord Chancellor, he became Baron Dilhorne. Per tradition
his Inn, the Inner Temple, gave a celebratory dinner and *an
ancient bencher asked: 'Who's the new Chancellor?' and was told
'Dilhorne.' The aged one responded: 'Thank God it's not that bloody
fool Manningham-Buller.'*

Nineteen years earlier in 1943 Sir Miles Lampson Bt.,
the British ambassador to Egypt from 1936 to 1946, was
elevated to the peerage as Baron Killearn. 'Not long afterwards a visitor lunching with the ambassador and his wife
said: 'It's so nice you're here now and not those Lampsons
whom everybody disliked so much.'[422]

This story is surely as old as English nomenclature, an example of which is Miss Hester Alington who became successively Lady Dunglass, Countess of Home, Lady Douglas-Home and finally Lady Home of The Hirsel making five names in all, which, as she complained, 'Seems a bit unfair as I've only ever been married to one man.'

Donald Trelford, *see* Private Eye

Anthony Trollope (1815–82), the Victorian novelist of whom Henry James said in *Partial Portraits*: 'His first, his inestimable merit was a complete appreciation of the usual.'

Trollope passed on the advice: *'Don't wash your dirty linen in public'* in *The Last Chronicle of Barset*, but he was only turning round the old French injunction *'Il faut laver son linge sale en famille'*, or 'One should wash one's dirty linen in private.' The important thing, surely, is to wash it before the dirt is noticeable.

St Vincent Troubridge, *see* Winston L. S. Churchill

Harry S. Truman (1884–1972) thirty-third president of the United States, 1945–52.

Commentators, especially the press, always cite Truman as someone who 'grew in office' when he entered the White House after Franklin Roosevelt's death. This was a convenient cover for the fact that they had all either ignored or underestimated the vice-president. Even as a senator from Missouri, Truman was always the tough political operator epitomized by his famous phrase: *'If you can't stand the heat, get out of the kitchen.'* The axiom is not Truman's. It has been assigned to Major-General Harry Vaughan[423] but probably predates both of them. What Truman actually said was 'If you can't stand the smell, get out of the shit-house.'[424]

Nor did Truman coin the motto '*the buck stops here*', he merely had it on a hand-lettered sign on his desk. '*Give 'em hell*' is not a Truman instruction: what he said to his running mate, Alben Barkly, in his 1948 re-election campaign, was: 'I'm going to fight hard. I'm going to give 'em hell',[425] but later he declared: 'I never give them hell. I just tell the truth, and they think it is hell.'[426] *See also* Herbert Hoover, General Douglas MacArthur *and* Groucho Marx.

Mark Twain (Samuel Langhorne Clemens, 1835–1910), American author and humorist.

Mark Twain merely had to quote other writers' work and then let posterity do the rest. Thus '*There are three kinds of lies: lies, damned lies and statistics*' is attributed by Twain to Disraeli and has ever since been wrongfully ascribed to Twain – or not. Nobody has been able to find any source for this remark other than Twain. (Statisticians prefer New York Mayor Fiorello La Guardia's 'Statistics are like alienists – they will testify for either side.')[427]

Fellow-humorist Edgar Wilson ('Bill' Nye) also lost one to Twain in '*Wagner's music is better than it sounds*', as did Charles Dudley Warner, the journalist who wrote in 1897: '*Everybody talks about the weather, but nobody does anything about it.*'[428] To his credit, Twain never claimed any of the above. Twain, perhaps, offered an explanation as to why people misquote with his description of a 'classic' book: '*Something that everybody wants to have read and nobody wants to read.*' That wasn't one of Twain's either: 'It's a classic, just as Professor Caleb Winchester says, and it meets his definition of a classic – something that everybody wants to have read and nobody wants to read.'[429]

Sometimes Twain's remarks were attributed to others. Back in 1894 Twain's *Puddenhead Wilson* gave the advice: 'Put all your eggs in one basket — and watch that basket.' Years later a journalist asked Andrew Carnegie, the steel millionaire, the secret of making a lot of money; he quoted Twain and was thenceforth given credit for inventing the remark. Carnegie blessed the world by providing it with hundreds of public libraries. Honour his memory. *See also* Sir Robert Armstrong, Hilaire Belloc, Will Rogers *and* George Washington.

U

Vladimir Ilyitch Ulyanov, *see* Lenin

V. V. Ulrikh, one of Josef Stalin's chief show-trial judges, was not a delightful personality. 'A fat man, with dewlaps like a bloodhound and little pig eyes. His shaven head rose to a point. His neck bulged over the collar of his uniform. His voice was soft and oily. He had much experience in political cases.'[430] His only remembered phrase is: '*Every man is guilty until proved innocent.*' He never made the remark and didn't need to. In his court nobody was proved innocent.

V

Vivian van Damm (?1889–1960), theatrical impresario.

Mr van Damm ran the Windmill Theatre in Soho. He introduced 'continuous review' with shows running from 2 p.m. to midnight. It was the only London theatre to remain open throughout the War, totally ignoring the bombing and the Blitz. Hence the proud slogan, '*We never closed*' (and because the shows were risqué this was sometimes changed to 'We never clothed'). But as Mr van Damm said in his autobiography: 'I did not coin the slogan. It was merely a statement of fact.'[431] He just adopted the admiring demotic '**They** never closed.' (It would be unsporting to mention that the Windmill never closed because it was London's only theatre small enough to escape the regulations that forced the others to shut when air raids were imminent.)

Queen Victoria (1819–1901), should have become Queen Alexandrina but chose to use her second name. Her son, Prince Albert, became Edward VII; one grandson was always known as David and so became Edward VIII while another, Prince Albert and always known as Bertie, became George VI.

All biographies and memoirs proving that, in private, Queen Victoria enjoyed jokes and jollity cannot wipe out her apocryphal comment '*We Are Not Amused*' (usually quoted with the capital letters pronounced) when a courtier told a risqué story. Alan Hardy, when researching *Queen Victoria Was Amused*,[432] could find no better evidence for the rebuke than the Victorian equivalent of Sunday tabloid's 'Exclusive!!!' – such as Arthur Beavan's *Popular Royalty* or the anonymous *Notebooks Of A Spinster Lady*.[433] Admiral Maxse was one man named as the culprit, but his daughter doubted he ever even met the Queen. J. A. Fuller Maitland in *A Doorkeeper Of Music* claimed the Hon. 'Alick' (Alexander) Yorke earned the rebuke after Victoria insisted on hearing his impersonation of herself. As the remark became firmly embedded in the national folk memory there were many who claimed it had been made to a parent to close relative – but 'twas ever thus.[434] *See also* Anon., Lewis Carroll, Benjamin Disraeli *and* Alfred, Lord Tennyson.

Voltaire (Jean-Marie Arouet, 1694–1778), French philosopher. If Voltaire had not said '*I disapprove of what you say, but I will defend to the death your right to say it*', it would have been necessary to invent it. He didn't. It was.

In 1758 another French philosopher, Claude Helvétius, published *De l'esprit*, a somewhat *jejune* work arguing that selfishness and passion are the wellsprings of human behaviour and that vice and virtue do not exist. The book was denounced by the Pope, criticized by the Sorbonne and in 1758 condemned by the French parliament to be burned by the public hangman. Upon hearing of this Voltaire exclaimed: '*What a fuss about an omelette*', if you believe James Parker;[435] some don't. S. G. Tallentyre writing in 1907 suggested Voltaire's attitude was: 'I disapprove of what you say, but I will defend to the death your right to say it' without ever claiming he used those words. Liberals have been using the phrase ever since – usually as a means of flaunting their liberal credentials.[436]

While Voltaire said: 'If God did not exist it would be necessary to invent him' ('*Si Dieu n'existait pas, il faudrait* *l'inventer*'[437]) the idea is as old as God. Some even debate which came first. John Tillotson (1630–94), Archbishop of Canterbury for the last three years of his life, said: 'As Tully* admirably says: *'Dei immortales ad usam hominum fabricati pene videantur* – If God were not a necessary Being of Himself, he might almost seem to be made for the use and benefit of men.'[438] Two thousand years earlier Euripides, 480–406 BC, suggested: 'He was a wise man who first invented God.' This remark has also been attributed to Plato and Aeschines.[439] The Almighty has not spoken on the matter but we might ponder the graffito '"God is dead – Nietzsche". "Nietzsche is dead – God".' Nietzsche's remark is unproven; God's remark is proved beyond argument. The caveat in Nietzsche's remark is largely unknown: 'God is dead, but looking at the way man is, there will probably be caves for thousands of years to come in which his shadow can be seen.'[440] *See also* Napoleon Bonaparte.

W

Sir Robert Walpole (1st Earl of Orford, 1676–1745) British statesman and prime minister, 1715–17 and 1721–42.

Sir Robert ran an efficient administration and, of course, did so by the customs of the day. He is wrongly remembered as saying *'All men have their price'*, or correctly 'All **those** men have their price.'[441] He was talking of some Opposition MPs who were parading their patriotism as good reason for

* Marcus Tullius Cicero, better known as 'Cicero', 106–43 BC.

opposing Walpole. The prime minister's dry remark was aimed at a specific group of individuals — it was not meant to be the general statement it has become. Walpole denied ever making the remark, but then 'He would say that, wouldn't he?'[442]

Sir Robert's youngest son, Horace, diarist and dilettante, invented the word 'serendipity' by happy accident. *See also* William Pitt, the Elder

Charles Dudley Warner, *see* Mark Twain

Dr John Watson, *see* Sherlock Holmes

George Washington (1732–99), American general and first president of the United States of America, 1789–97.

The childhood tale of little George and the cherry tree has taken on the monumentality of a fable by Aesop, but is conveniently without a moral — other than lying is best left to those with a talent for it. There are two well-known versions: in Mason Locke Weems's biography, Washington is apprehended in the act and after some consideration, decides it prudent to confess: '*I can't tell a lie, Pa; you know I can't tell a lie. I did cut it with my hatchet.*' There is also the slightly more facetious version by Mark Twain: '*Father, I cannot tell a lie. I did it with my little hatchet.*' In both cases, Washington's vandal streak and his seeming inability to prevaricate (the former an augur of his later military career and the latter a prophecy — what kind of general cannot bluff?) is lauded by his father who congratulates his six-year-old son for his 'act of heroism'.[443]

Washington said on his deathbed: 'Doctor, I die hard, but I am not afraid to go', but he did not add '*Bring me the Book*':[444] more sensibly 'Let me go quietly. I cannot last long.'[445] Christians also attributed to him: '*It is impossible to rightly govern the world without God and the Bible,*' but the rationalists pinned on him '*The government of the United States is not in any sense founded upon the Christian religion.*' The first is nowhere in his speeches or published writings. The latter is merely part of a good-mannered preamble from an agreement which the American consul in Algiers, Joel Barlow, signed with the local Moslem authorities.[446] In his lifetime Washington showed no interest in Christianity beyond that required to avoid comment when such beliefs were expected of a gentleman.

'Contrary to what ninety-eight per cent of those who cite it believe, the phrase warning the United States against "entangling alliances" is not from George Washington's Farewell Address but from Thomas Jefferson's First Inaugural Address. It is all too typical of Jefferson in its fuzzy-mindedness. All alliances worth anything entangle. The trick is to ensure that the entanglement is worth the candle. Washington understood this and therefore warned against "permanent alliances" entered into and maintained for the wrong reasons – for example, sentiment – which would not withstand scrutiny from statesmen moved by honourable self-interest (oxymoron?).

'Of course, Washington's Farewell Address is never cited because it is never read. And it is never read because "It is too pointed a criticism of aspects of contemporary US foreign policy which our leaders would rather not acknowledge – even to themselves." So wrote a friend in the American Foreign Service. The actual quotations are:

'Equal and exact justice to all men of whatever state
or persuasion, religious or political; peace, commerce,
and honest friendship with all nations, entangling

156

alliances with none ...' Thomas Jefferson, First Inaugural Address, 4 March 1801.

'It is our policy to steer clear of permanent alliances with any portion of the foreign world.' George Washington, Farewell Address, 17 September 1776.

John Wayne (Marion Michael Morrison, 1907–79), American film star who never acted a role out of character – his character.

'*A man's gotta do what a man's gotta do.*' This manly if equivocal philosophy was not a Marion Michael Morrison original, nor did it appear as dialogue in any of his eighty-plus films. It only felt that way. The original comes, in a slightly different form, from the A. B. Guthrie screenplay of the archetypal western *Shane* (1953). Shane, as portrayed by the vertically challenged[447] actor Alan Ladd, advises the chronologically deprived child star Brandon de Wilde, that 'A man has to be what he is, Joey', which is a much kinder, gentler observation than the first. It is a woman character in the film who later reintroduces the stoicism and absolutism of the misquote by saying: 'Shane did what he had to do.' Wayne scored a near miss in *Hondo* (1953) with 'A man ought to do what he thinks is right', from the screenplay by James Edward Grant based on a short story by Louis L'Amour. John Steinbeck came closest in *The Grapes of Wrath*: 'I know this – a man got to do what he got to do.'[448]

Mason Locke Weems, *see* George Washington

Sidney and Beatrice Webb (Lord and Lady Passfield), *see* Lenin *and* Lincoln Steffens

Johnny Weissmuller, *see* Edgar Rice Burroughs

Orson Welles, *see* Winston L. S. Churchill *and* Graham Greene

Arthur Wellesley, 1st Duke of Wellington (1769–1852) who, 'as every schoolboy knows', said: '*The battle of Waterloo was won on the playing-fields of Eton.*' He didn't; it wasn't.

The story began with one Count de Montalembert visiting England three years after Wellington died, and reporting that when the Duke visited his old College, he said: '*C'est ici qu'a été gagné la bataille de Waterloo*'[449] – 'It is here that the battle of Waterloo was won.' A little later, Sir Edward Creasy wrote that Wellington, passing the playing-fields of Eton, remarked: 'There grows the stuff that won Waterloo.'[450] Then, in 1889, Sir William Frazer finally gave the world the vapid phrase it has loved ever since.[451] The Duke had no affection for his old school; he had not been happy there, and in his schooldays at Eton the college did not have playing-fields.[452]

The iron Duke was particularly susceptible to misquotation. He was not in the habit of repeating himself, and: '*I always say that, next to a battle lost, the greatest misery is a battle gained*', is garbled tosh.[453] He may well have replied to the statement 'What a glorious thing must be a victory, Sir', with the umambiguous 'The greatest tragedy in the world, Madam, except a defeat'.[454] He did remark: 'The next greatest misfortune to losing a battle is to gain a victory such as this',[455] which is understandable as he was referring to Waterloo: 'It has been a damn serious business – Blucher and I have lost 30,000 men.'[456] The Battle of Waterloo should be called the battle of La Haye Sainte, which is where Wellington had his centre. The little village of Waterloo was 'half a league away' (about one and a half miles distant). The Germans refer to the event as the battle of La Belle Alliance, while the French hardly refer to it at all.[457]

Wellington did not comment on the newly drafted troops, arriving in the Peninsula in 1810: '*I don't know what effect they'll have on the enemy, but, by God, they frighten me.*' This is a corruption of His Grace quoting, with attribution, a remark of the 4th Earl of Chesterfield. 'When I reflect upon the characters and attainments of some of the general officers of this army, and consider that these are the persons on whom I am to rely to lead columns against the French, I tremble; and as Lord Chesterfield said of the generals of his day, "I only hope that when the enemy reads the list of their names, he trembles as I do."' Nor did he say: '*Up, Guards, and at 'em*', as Captain Batty claimed, but 'Up Guards. Make ready.' Neither did he call Waterloo '*A damned close-run thing*' ('It has been a damned nice thing – the nearest run thing you ever saw in your life.'). Equally spurious is '*The Queen's government must be carried on*' ('What is the best to be done for the country? How is the Queen's government to be carried on?').[458]

However he almost certainly did write 'Publish and be damned' to the courtesan Miss Harriette Wilson. This enterprising lady was offering her former paramours the option of buying themselves out of her forthcoming autobiography, which began with the never-bettered opening line: 'I shall not say how and why I became, at the age of fifteen, the mistress of the Earl of Craven.'[459]

While Miss Wilson's opening line has never been bettered, it was equalled by an idle undergraduate. Asked by his tutor what he had done during his three years at university, he was reluctant to say 'Nothing.' Struck by inspiration he replied: 'I've written a novel, Sir.' The tutor asked to see it; the student demurred, 'You wouldn't like it.' The don responded: 'How can you know whether I'll like it?' 'Well,' replied the slacker, 'the first sentence is: 'Mabel's naked body quivered in ecstatic anticipation of the descending lash.' Which was not only the first sentence of the novel but the only sentence. Anthony Hartley gave this story to Bernard Levin who gave it to Godfrey Smith who used it in his *Sunday Times* column.[460] *See also* Stanley Baldwin *and* Francis I.

H. G. (Herbert George) Wells, *see* David Lloyd George (*under* 'G')

Revd John Wesley, *see* the Bible *and* Rabbi Phineas Ben Yair

Miss Mae West (1892?–1980) was, is and always will be Miss Mae West. All her hundreds of impersonators are nothing but impersonators.

As Miss West pointed out: 'I'm never dirty. I'm just interesting without being vulgar. I just ... suggest.' And there's enough suggestion in '*Is that a gun in your pocket, or are you just pleased to see me?*', to arouse the most jaded male ego, although her actual remark was: 'Is that your sword, or are you just pleased to see me?'. That was an example of her spontaneous wit, occurring during a period play in New York when her co-star got his sword tangled up in his cloak.[461]

In her film *She Done Him Wrong* (1933), Miss West said to a young Cary Grant: 'Why don't you come up sometime and see me.' Say that tongue-twister three times swiftly and you will realize why her multitude of fans prefer the apocryphal version, '*Come up and see me sometime.*' Miss West co-authored her 1940 film *My Little Chickadee* with her co-star, W. C. Fields, and the amended line occurs in the script – but the joke is that Fields, not West, says it.[462] Miss West also paraphrased Ben Jonson (q.v.): 'Keep thy shop and thy shop will keep thee'[463] when she said 'Keep a diary and someday it will keep you.'[464] *See also* W. C. Fields *and* Alexander Woollcott.

T. K. Whipple, *see* Theodore Dreiser

James (Abbott) MacNeil Whistler (1834–1903), *see* Paul Jones

Oscar Wilde (1854–1900), Irish wit, playwright, poet and (unbeknown to himself) pioneer gay rights campaigner.

'*Work is the curse of the drinking classes*' is a classic Wilde aphorism, but the earliest trace of it is in Mr Hesketh Pearson's 1946 biography of the great aesthete[465] – thus being too late to appear in Mr Pearson's *Common Misquotations*, published twelve years before. This epigram turns round the old temperance reproof: 'Drink is the curse of the working classes', but that saw is absent from all the volumes of quotations I have consulted. So either compilers of such books have long been an egalitarian crowd, or a bibulous one.

Oscar Wilde's dying words have been variously reported as: '*Ah well, then I suppose I shall have to die beyond my means*', upon hearing the fee required for an operation.[466] Or, on ordering another bottle of champagne: '*Alas, I am dying as I have lived, beyond my means.*'[467] Or, on a different tack altogether: '*Either that wallpaper goes, or I do.*'[468] No more than one of those can be right: I opt for the wallpaper.

I hope it's true that Wilde, when at Niagara and asked

by some local worthies if he did not think the Falls impressive, replied: *'They would be more impressive if they ran the other way'*, but I can't trace him doing so.

Wilde said: 'There is no sin, except stupidity', and if you've read this book thus far you'll agree with him. If you're just dipping and disagree with him, give this book to someone whose good opinion you seek. *See also* John Paul Jones.

Kaiser Wilhelm II (1859–1941), last emperor of Germany. At the outbreak of the Great War a small British Expeditionary Force (the BEF) was sent to France and shortly thereafter, on 24 September 1914, the following Orders of the Day were issued:

The following is a copy of orders issued by the German Emperor on August 19th:

It is my Royal and Imperial Command that you concentrate your energies, for the immediate present, upon one single purpose, and that is that you address all your skill and all the valour of my soldiers to exterminate first the treacherous English and to walk over General French's contemptible little army.

Headquarters, Aix La Chapelle, August 19th

The results of the orders were the operations commencing with Mons and the advance of the seemingly overwhelming masses against us. The answer of the British army as the subject of extermination has already been given.

Printing Co., Royal Engineers 69

Which infuriated the troops of the BEF. Wilhelm's apologists later explained that Wilhelm did not denigrate the BEF as his phrase was *'a contemptibly little army'*. Such is the difference changing one vowel can make.

In fact the explanation is as bogus as the original quotation. That Order of the Day was made up in its entirety by British propaganda officers and German headquarters were never at Aix. After the War, Major-General Sir Frederick Maurice asked the Kaiser, at Doorn in Holland, if he had ever used such a phrase. His Majesty – a grandson of Queen Victoria and (until August 1914) a British Admiral of the Fleet, Field Marshal and Colonel-in-Chief of the 1st Royal Dragoons – said he had never done so, adding: 'On the contrary. I continually emphasized the high quality of the British army and often gave warning against underestimating them.'[469] After the war, the veterans of the BEF took up the phrase and called themselves 'The Old Contemptibles'. *See also* John Barnes.

Charles E. Wilson (1890–1961), president and chief executive of General Motors Inc., and later President Eisenhower's Secretary of Defence.

At his Senate confirmation hearings, Wilson was asked what he would do if he had to take a decision that would benefit America as a whole but hurt General Motors, in which he remained a major stockholder. An ever vigilant press reported his answer the next day: *'What's good for General Motors is good for the USA.'* (This has also been attributed to Alfred P. Sloan Jr. (1875–1966), author of *My Life With General Motors*.)

Wilson actually replied that he could not conceive of having to take such a decision because 'For years I thought that what was good for our country was good for General Motors, and vice versa.'[470] Balanced remarks do not make a good story nor, equally important, a good headline.

Edgar Wilson ('Bill' Nye), *see* Mark Twain

(James) Harold Wilson (Lord Wilson of Rievaulx, 1916–95), British prime minister, 1964–70 and 1974–76.

Wilson pandered to the media and for several years enjoyed an overindulgent Press. In a speech on 1 October 1963 to Labour's annual conference, he was reported as promising that Labour would create '*a Britian forged in the white heat of the technological revolution*'. The sentiment, as Wilson expressed it, was more verbose: 'We are redefining and restating our socialism in terms of the scientific revolution. . . . the Britain that is going to be forged in the white heat of this revolution will be no place for restrictive practices or outdated methods on either side of industry.'[471]

Wilson claimed he had been misrepresented, and that he had not said in a radio broadcast on 19 November 1967 that '*The pound in your pocket has not been devalued.*' His actual words were: 'From now the pound abroad is worth fourteen per cent or so less than in terms of other currencies. It does not mean, of course, that the pound here in Britain, in your pocket or purse or in your bank, has been devalued.' A fair summary of that is, surely, 'The pound in your pocket has not been devalued.'

John Wilson, *see under* his pen-name Christopher North

Woodrow Wilson (1856–1924), twenty-eighth president of the United States, 1913–21, and main architect of the Versailles Peace Treaty. He did not get on well with France's

Georges Clemenceau who said of him: 'How can I talk to a fellow who thinks himself the first man in two thousand years to know anything about peace on earth?'[472]

When William Safire used the words '*With healing in its wings*', he put them between inverted commas to indicate it was a quotation (from, he thought, Woodrow Wilson). But when Wilson used the words at the beginning of the century he did not put them in quotation marks, as they are from the Bible and he could be assured, therefore, that his listeners would know them. The 'author' is the prophet Malachi. 'But unto you that fear my name shall the sun of righteousness arise with healing in its wings.'[473] This tells us how far Christianity has advanced in America over the last ninety years. Sir Julian Huxley noted: 'Operationally, God is beginning to resemble not a ruler but the last fading smile of a cosmic Cheshire cat.'[474] Saki, of all unlikely people, offers comfort: 'People may say what they like about the decay of Christianity; but the religious system that produced green chartreuse can never really die.'[475] *See also* David Lloyd George.

Professor Caleb Winchester, *see* Mark Twain

His Royal Highness The Duke of Windsor (1894–1972), remittance-man. The charismatic charm of the man who was briefly King Edward VIII concealed nothing, for underneath there was nothing to conceal. On a visit to South Wales in 1936 he saw the Dowlais iron and steel works which had been closed, throwing many men out of work. He did not then say '*Something must be done*' but, less incisively and more characteristically, 'Something should be done.'[476] But when he got back to London, possessing all the prestige and influence of the throne, he did nothing.[477]

Her Grace The Duchess of Windsor (née Wallis Warfield 1896?–1986) drew several of life's short straws. No one has ever traced her birth certificate; her father died of tuberculosis when she was only a few months old, and her first husband was an alcoholic. Expecting to be Queen of England, she was forced by circumstances to marry an ex-king just when she was starting to become bored with him – and then they had thirty-five years of married life together. Her brother-in-law, George VI, would not allow her the style 'Her Royal Highness' (which even the fun-loving Sarah Ferguson was granted on her marriage to HRH Prince Andrew). Her only alleged aphorism is *'You can't be too rich or too thin'*, but Jonathon Green could not trace it back earlier than 1958 when that real American Queen, Truman Capote, said it wistfully on David Susskind's television chat show.[478]

Catherine Winkworth, *see* General Sir Charles Napier

William Wirt, *see* Patrick Henry

George Wither (1588–1667) never quite managed to turn his coat at the right moment from Royalist to Parliamentarian and back again. Sentenced to death by Charles I he was saved by Sir John Denham, who pleaded 'that so long as Wither live I shall not be accounted the worst poet in England'.[479] Wither sneaks into this book because of that story, but qualifies because he wrote 'And I oft have heard defended/Little said is soonest mended',[480] which *hoi polloi* have trimmed to *'Least said, soonest mended.'*

P. G. Wodehouse (Sir Pelham Grenville Wodehouse, 1881–1975), Anglo-American comic writer and lyricist. Creator of Bertie Wooster, his valet Jeeves, Lord Emsworth and others.

In 1926 Wodehouse dedicated *The Heart Of A Goof*, his second book of golfing stories, '*To my daughter Leonora, without whose never-failing sympathy and encouragement this book would have been finished in half the time*', but that was not original. He was quoting himself, for in the first edition of his *A Gentleman Of Leisure* appears the dedication: 'To Herbert Westbrook, without whose never-failing sympathy and encouragement this book would have been finished in half the time.' Westbrook was charming but idle, a colleague of Wodehouse's on *The Globe*, a London evening paper. Later editions of *A Gentleman Of Leisure* were dedicated to Douglas Fairbanks Sr. who starred in the play of the book.[481]

Wodehouse gave many words and phrases to the English that are so common we take them to be of ancient provenance – phrases such as 'Down to earth', 'loony-bin' and 'dirty work at the crossroads'.[482] But he did not coin '*a stiff upper lip*', which his scholarly friend and fellow lyricist Ira Gershwin traced back to the *Massachusetts Spy* of 1815.[483] *See also* Francis Bacon *and* Ben Jonson.

John Wolcot (pen-name Peter Pindar), *see* George M. Cohan

Charles Wolf Jr., *see* Karl Marx

Humbert Wolfe, *see* Hilaire Belloc

Tom Wolfe (1931–), is the author of *The Bonfire Of The Vanities*, usually misquoted as *Bonfire Of Vanities*, a novel of New York. Few places are more suitable for a bonfire of the vanities than New York – and in fewer places is it less likely to happen. The original bonfire of the vanities occurred in Florence, under the zealot monk Savonarola, when ladies threw all their sumptuous finery into the public square to be burned. (Well, maybe not quite all of it.)

Alexander Woollcott (1887–1943) was a frequenter of the Algonquin Round Table whose members were eminently quotable, if nothing else.

Woollcott, Grand Pooh-bah of the 'Vicious Circle', is given credit for '*I must get out of these wet clothes and into a dry Martini.*'[484] Why this has been attributed to Mr Woollcott is unclear, since the line was first made prominent by fellow-member Robert Benchley in a film, *The Major and the Minor*, in 1942. Benchley himself took the line from his press agent.[485] However, Mae West used it in *Every Day's A Holiday* in 1937. The joke is as old as the dry Martini which, the company tells me, is as old as the century. *See also* Dorothy Parker.

X

Xenophanes (*c.* 570–480 BC), Greek philosopher. His most noted aphorism is: '*It takes a wise man to recognize a wise man*'.[486] The earliest source for his remark is Diogenes Laertius, writing in the second century AD in his *Great Philosophers*, which Chambers says is 'worthless in respect of plan or criticism'.[487]

Y

Rabbi Phineas Ben Yair (*c.* 150–200), Jewish sage.

Ben Yair devised a 'ladder to saintliness'. 'Caution against evil leads to eagerness for good. Eagerness to cleanliness, cleanliness to purity, purity to asceticism, asceticism to holiness, holiness to humility, humility to fear of God, fear of God to attainment of the Holy Spirit and attainment of the Holy Spirit to resurrection of the dead.'[488] John Wesley, the founder of Methodism, took part of that idea in a sermon 'On Dress': 'Slovenliness is no part of religion; neither this nor any text in scripture condemns neatness of apparel. Certainly this is a duty, not a sign. Cleanliness is, indeed, next to Godliness.'[489] The common summary of that, '*Cleanliness is next to godliness*', doesn't quite convey the full depth of meaning of the original or even of Wesley's extract from it. The sentiment, as such, does not appear anywhere in the Bible (q.v.) although the Book of Common Prayer (1662) enjoins worshippers to be 'cleanly, soberly and decently dressed'. The Koran tells the faithful that 'God loveth the clean.'[490]

Yale University, Newport, Connecticut, can boast above the door of its Hall of Graduate Studies the inscription: '*Born with the gift of laughter and a sense that the world was mad.*' This was assumed to be by some savant of old until the architect, John D. Tuttle, confessed in a letter to *The New Yorker* on 8 December 1934 that the line was by Rafael Sabatini, describing the swashbuckling hero of his novel *Scaramouche*. The elders of Yale were not amused, and ivy was carefully trained to cover the offending inscription – as it does to this day.[491•]

Z

General Gregoriy Yevseyevich Zinoviev (1883–1936). Proselytizing Communist, murdered by is friend Stalin.

In their early years Russian Communists went in for name-changes and grand job descriptions. Vladimir Ilich Ulyanov became Lenin, Yosef Vissarionovich Dzhugashvili became Stalin ('steel') and Lev Davidovich Bronstein became Leon Trotsky. Zinoviev, born Radomysiskiy, rejoiced in the title 'President of the Presidium of the Third International' and was responsible for spreading Communision in Europe and America.

In December 1923 American Secretary of State, Charles Hughes, released the text of instructions Zinoviev had sent to the Workers Party of America: '*We hope the Party will step by step embrace the proletarian forces of America, and in the not too distant future raise the red flag over the White House*' and the newspapers, even the staid *New York Times*, had a field day.

Next year, in the middle of a general election, the British press had their turn with the publication of the Zinoviev Letter on 25 October 1924. The irrepressible general declared: '*Armed warfare must be preceded by a struggle against the inclinations to compromise which are embedded among the majority of British workmen, against the idea of evolution and peaceful extermination of capitalism. Only then will it be possible to count upon complete success of an armed insurrection.*'[492] The Zinoviev Letter was credited, quite wrongly, with losing the election for the Labour government (which actually won a million more votes, an increase of over a quarter).

Both communications were counterfeit. The 'instructions' were forged by the predecessor to the FBI and the 'Zinoviev Letter' by a group of Polish *émigrés* aiming to sabotage an Anglo-Soviet trade agreement (they succeeded). The odd thing is that Zinoviev had, genuinely, issued similar hortations before, to both countries, and they had been treated as the tedious rantings of an extremist.

Admiral Elmo R. Zumwait, *see* Henry Kissinger. When Chief of US Naval Operations the admiral would send brief, concise memos which were models of clarity. These became known as 'Z-grams'.

The moral of this work is:

Caveat lector

The motto of compilers of quotations is:

'*If you steal from one author it's plagiarism;
if you steal from many it's research.*'[493]

FREQUENTLY CITED
AND CONSULTED SOURCES

A. S. E. Ackerman *Popular Fallacies*, 4th edn, London, Old Westminster Press, 1950

Tony Augarde *The Oxford Dictionary of Modern Quotations*, Oxford, Oxford University Press, 1992

John Bartlett *Familiar Quotations*, London, George Routledge & Sons, 1887

John Bartlett (ed. Christopher Morley) *Familiar Quotations*, London, Macmillan, 1937

John Bartlett (ed. Emily Morison Beck) *Familiar Quotations*, London, Macmillan, 1980

Sir Gurney Benham *Benham's Quotations*, 1948 edn London, John G. Harrap. NB page columns are identified 'a' and 'b'.

Nicholas Bentley & Evan Esar *The Treasury of Humorous Quotations*, London, Aldine Paperbacks, 1962

Paul F. Boller Jr. & John George *They Never Said It*, New York, Oxford University Press, 1989

E. Cobham Brewer *The Dictionary of Phrase and Fable*, 1894 edn, reprinted 1978, New York, Avenal; *Brewer's Twentieth Century Dictionary of Phrase and Fable* London, Cassell, 1991

Tom Burnham *Dictionary of Misinformation: the Book to Set the Record Straight*, New York, Ballantyne, 1975; *More Misinformation*, New York, Ballantyne, 1980

J. M. & M. J. Cohen *The Penguin Dictionary of Quotations*, London, Penguin, 1960; *The Penguin Dictionary of Modern Quotations*, revised edn, Harmondsworth, Penguin, 1976; *The New Penguin Dictionary of Quotations*, London, Viking, 1992

Nicholas Comfort *Brewer's Politics*, London, Cassell, 1993

Henry Davidoff (ed.) *The Pocket Book of Quotations*, Cardinal edn, New York, Pocket Books Inc., 1959

Isaac D'Israeli, *Curiosities Of Literature*, one-vol. edn, undated, London, George Routledge, c. 1870

Jonathon Green *Says Who?*, London, Longmans, 1988

Sir Paul Harvey *The Oxford Companion to English Literature*, revised edn, Oxford, Oxford University Press, 1933

Robert Hendrickson *The Literary Life and Other Curiosities*, Harmondsworth, Penguin, 1982; *The Facts On File Encyclopedia of Word and Phrase Origins*, New York and Oxford, Facts On File, 1987

Simon James *A Dictionary of Economic Quotations*, 2nd edn, London, Croom Helm, 1984; *A Dictionary of Sexist Quotations*, Brighton, Harvest Press, 1984

Colin Jarman (compiler) *I Said It My Way*, London, Guinness Publishing, 1994

W. Francis H. King *Classical and Foreign Quotations*, London, J. Whitaker & Sons, 1914

Frank Magill *Quotations in Context*, Harper & Row, 1965 and second series 1969

H. L. Mencken *A New Dictionary of Quotations*, New York, Alfred A. Knopf, 1982

Alan & Veronica Palmer *A Dictionary of Historical Quotations*, revised edn, London, Paladin, 1985

Hesketh Pearson *Common Misquotations*, London, Hamish Hamilton, 1934

Stephen Pile *The Book of Heroic Failures* London, Futura, 1980

The Oxford Dictionary Of Quotations, 1942, 2nd imp. revised, Oxford, Oxford University Press; 1985, 3rd edn corrected, Oxford, Oxford University Press

Mark Rogers *Contradictory Quotations*, Harlow, Longman, 1983

Burton Stevenson *The Home Book of Quotations*, 10th edn, New York, Dodd Mead, 1967

J. O. Thorne (ed.) *Chambers Biographical Dictionary*, revised edn, Edinburgh, W & R Chambers, 1972

Rhoda Thomas Tripp *Penguin International Thesaurus of Quotations*, Harmondsworth, Penguin, 1976

Michael Upshall (ed.) *The Hutchinson Encyclopedia*, 1978 edn, London, Hutchinson.

Philip Ward *A Dictionary of Common Fallacies*, 2 vols., 2nd edn, Cambridge and New York, Cambridge University Press and Oleander, 1980

Justin Wintle & Richard Kenin *The Penguin Concise Dictionary of Bioigraphical Quotations*, Harmondsworth, Penguin, 1981; *The Dictionary of Biographical Quotation*, New York, Dorset Press, 1989

INDEX OF KEY WORDS
AND PHRASES

The index below shows the entries where phrases
and subjects can be found. The correct authors
are given within those entries.

A contemptible little army	Kaiser Wilhelm II
A damned close-run thing	Wellington
A horse, a horse	Shakespeare
A land fit for heroes	George, David Lloyd
A little knowledge	Pope
A lost generation	Stein
A man's gotta do	Wayne
A rose is a rose is a rose	Stein
A stiff upper lip	Wodehouse
A Woman of No Importance	Jones
accursed power, The	Belloc
Across the wires	Austin
Age before beauty	Parker
Alas!, poor Yorick	Shakespeare
Albion, perfidious	Napoleon
All human life is there	*News of the World*
All is lost save honour	Francis I
All men have their price	Walpole
All that glitters	Shakespeare

All that men need to know	Omar
All power corrupts	Acton
alliances	Washington
America/Americans	Henry, Jones, Kipling, Kissinger, Zinoviev
An honest God	Ingersoll
And yet it moves	Galileo
Any colour you like	Ford
Anyone who hates animals and kids	Fields
architecture	Charles, Prince of Wales
Army's Beatitude	Anon.
Art of the Possible	Butler, R. A.
Atrocious crime of being a young man	Pitt the Elder
Barabbas was a publisher	Byron
bastardy	Birkenhead
Beam me up, Scotty	Kirk
Bellamys' veal pies	Pitt the Younger
Best prime minister we have	Butler, R. A.
Better Red than dead	Russell
big battalions	Napoleon
Blessed is he	Anon.
blood, specific gravity of	Scott, Sir W.
Blood, toil, sweat and tears	Churchill
Bonfire of Vanities	Wolfe
books	Gibbon, Ingersoll, Morris, Omar, Twain
Brandy for heroes	Johnson, Dr S.
Buck stops here	Truman
Bugger Bognor	George V
Build a better mousetrap	Emerson

bunk, bunkum	Roosevelt, F. D.
business of America, The	Coolidge
But for the grace of God	Churchill
Caviar to the general	Shakespeare
certainty	Disraeli
cheating	Disraeli
Chicken in every pot	Hoover
chickens	Butler, S., Lytton
Christianity	Wilson, W.
Church of England	Disraeli
cigars	Churchill
class distinctions	Belloc, Curzon
cleanliness	Curzon, Yair
clichés	Armstrong, Sir R.
Coals to Newcastle	Melville
cold war	Baruch
Come up and see me	West
Come wiz me to ze Kasbah	Boyer
communism	Capitalism, de Gaulle, Reagan, Roosevelt, F. D.; Russell
conscience	Disraeli
Conservative Party	Disraeli
consistency	Emerson
corruption	Acton, Agnew, Belloc, Harding, Kennedy
courage	Butler, S.; Shakespeare
cowards, cowardice	Butler, S.; Shakespeare
created/creation	Darwin, Jefferson
creeds	Athanasius
Crisis? What Crisis?	Callaghan
Cross of Lorraine	de Gaulle

Cuckoo clock	Greene
culture	Goering
curses	Lytton
Customer is always right	Ritz
Cut prices at a stroke	Heath
Damn with faint praise	Pope
Dead language	Gibbon
death, dying words	Austin, Beeton, Bible, Darwin, Disraeli, Duncan, George V, Henry, Introduction, Jones, Parker, Pitt the Younger, Quarles, Rowley, Washington, Wilde
dedications	Wodehouse
defeat is an orphan	Kennedy
dying words, see death	
dirty linen, washing policy	Trollope
discretion	Shakespeare
Don't count your chickens	Butler, S.
Don't fire until you see the whites of their eyes	Prescott
draft-dodger	Clinton
Drop the gun, Loui	Bogart
dumb son of a bitch	MacArthur
duty	Dickens
Economical with the truth	Armstrong, Sir R.
eggs in baskets, proportion	Twain
Elementary, my dear Watson	Holmes
embalmer's art	Reagan
Empire, British	George V, Kipling, North

English, the	Kipling, Napoleon
Enough to make a saint swear	Lowell
entangling alliances	Washington
equal/equality	Jefferson
Estates in Parliament	Burke
Eton, Battle of Waterloo at	Wellington
Every man is guilty	Ulrikh
Every schoolboy knows	Macaulay
Everything worth doing	Parker
evil	Burke
Exception proves the rule	Proverbial
Eternal vigilance	Jefferson
Father, I cannot tell a lie	Washington
Fellow immigrants	Roosevelt, F. D.
Fifth column	Franco
Fighting	Jones
fights	Butler, S.
Films	Agnew, Burroughs, Garbo, Goldwyn, Navarro, Parker
First catch your hare	Beeton
fishing	Johnson, Dr S.
Float like a butterfly	Ali
followers	Law
Fools rush in	Bible
Forgotten man	Roosevelt, F. D.
fragrance	Caulfield
fun-loving	Private Eye
General Motors	Wilson, C. E.
genius	Carlyle
Gentlemen and gents	Law
Germany is my spiritual home	Haldane

Gerry's the only man I know	Johnson, L. B.
Get on yer bike	Tebbit
Gild the lily	Shakespeare
give 'em hell	Truman
Give me a boy	Loyola
Go West, young man	Greeley
God	Bible, Churchill, Cromwell, Dickens, Ingersoll, Napoleon, Voltaire, Washington, Wilson W.
God is Dead	Voltaire
God tempers the wind	Bible
gold	Keynes, Shakespeare
good Americans	Jones
government	Washington
grandeur, delusions of	de Gaulle
great unwashed, The	Burke
green chartreuse	Wilson W.
Guards die but never surrender	de Cambronne
gun ownership	Lenin
Hang the Kaiser	Barnes
Hard-faced men	Baldwin
He governs best	Jefferson
Healing in its wings	Wilson, W.
Hell hath no fury	Congreve
Here I stand	Lincoln
Here's another fine mess	Hardy
heroism (see also brandy)	Kennedy
Hesitation	Addison
He that lives	Butler, S.
History is bunk	Ford
History repeats itself	Marx, K.

Hobgoblin of little minds	Emerson
homosexuality	Navarro, *Private Eye*
Honey, I forgot to duck	Reagan
I am Joan of Arc	Gaulle
I disapprove of what you say	Voltaire
I have not yet begun to fight	Jones
I have seen the future	Steffens
I have Sind/sinned	Napier
I never met a man I didn't like	Rogers
I rob banks	Sutton
I shall return	MacArthur
I want to be alone	Garbo
I wish I was as sure	Disraeli
If asked I will not stand	Sherman
If God did not exist	Voltaire
If I advance follow me	Mussolini
If I have seen farther	Newton
If the mountain	Bacon
If you can't stand the heat	Truman
Impossible to come. Lie follows	Proust
In the midst of life	Bible
In two words, 'im-possible'	Goldwyn
Include me out	Goldwyn
Indians, see native Americans	
Indebted to his memory	Sheridan R. B.
Indict a whole people	Burke
Intelligent people and intelligence	Law
Intemperance	Churchill, Johnson, Dr S.; Pitt the Younger
Is all well with the Empire?	George V
Is that a gun in your pocket	West
It doesn't matter what they say	Cohan

It is worse than a crime	Talleyrand
iron curtain, an	Churchill
jest/jokes	Miller, Sheridan, R. B.
justice	France
Keep a diary	West
Keep a shop	West
Know your lines	Coward, Tracy
Lady's not for turning, The	Thatcher
Lafayette, we are here	Pershing
Last refuge of a scoundrel	Bottomley
Latin language	Quayle
Law, in its majesty equality	France
Law of the Yukon	Darwin
Leaders	Law
Least said, soonest mended	Wither
Lebensraum	Hitler
lesbianism	Goldwyn
Let them eat cake	Marie-Antoinette
liberty	Acton, Henry, Lenin
Lies, inability to tell	Washington
lies and statistics	Twain
life	O'Malley
Like many of the Upper Class	Belloc
Lion for a day	Mussolini
Live to fight another day	Butler, S.
London	Austin
losing	Durocher
Mabel's naked body	Wellington
Madness	Shakespeare

Mahomet	Bacon
Martini, a dry	Woollcott
Marxism, Capitalism, Lenin	Marx, Groucho; Marx, Karl
Mass, a	Henri IV
Me Tarzan, you Jane	Burroughs
merciful man, A	Bible
Metathesis	Spooner
Method in his madness	Shakespeare
money	Bible, Coolidge, Gresham, Shaw
Monstrous carbuncle	Charles, Prince of Wales
Montezuma's revenge	Macaulay
Mother of Parliaments	Bright
Mousetraps, better	Emerson
Music hath charms	Congreve
My country right or wrong	Decatur
names, much about	Traditional
Naples	Byron
Nation shall speak peace	Reith
native Americans	Sheridan, P.
navigators, ablest	Napoleon
Neat not gaudy	Lamb
Next to a battle lost	Washington
Niagara Falls, unimpressive	Wilde
Nice guys finish last	Durocher
No man is a hero to his valet	de Sévigné
Noble experiment	Hoover
Not a penny off the pay	Cook
Not tonight Josephine	Ray
O rare Ben Jonson	Jonson
Off with his head	Shakespeare

Old Contemptibles	Wilhelm II
Old soldiers never die	MacArthur
officers, military	Clausewitz
pacifism	Oxford Union
Paddle your own canoe	Lincoln
Paris is well worth a Mass	Henri IV
patriotism	Bottomley, Decatur, Haldane, Johnson, Dr S.; Oxford Union, Pitt the Younger
Peace with honour	Francis I
Peccavi (I have sinned)	Napier
pens vs. swords	Lytton
Perfidious Albion	Napoleon
Philadelphia	Fields
Pissing out of the tent	Hoover
plagiarism	Churchill, Francis I, Jones
Play it again, Sam	Bogart
poetry	Austin, Malley, Nash, Wither
politics/politicians	Geddes, Keynes, Lincoln, Sherman
Portrait of Dorian Gray	Jones
Pound in your pocket	Wilson, H.
Pouring oil on troubled waters	Bible
power	Acton, Baldwin, Belloc
Power without responsibility	Baldwin
Praise the Lord and pass the ammunition	Maguire
Prerogative of the harlot	Baldwin
Press, The	Agnew, Baldwin, Belloc, Burke, Pitt the Elder
pride goeth before a fall	Bible
Professions are conspiracies	Shaw

Property is theft	Marx, K.
protection	Lincoln
public finance	Cicero
public taste	Murdoch
Publish and be damned	Wellington
publishers	Byron, Hennessy
Pursuit of happiness	Jefferson
Pyrenees no longer exist	Louis XIV
Queen's government must be carried on	Wellington
Race is not always to the swift	Napoleon
rejection slips	Stein
religion	Gibbon, Golden Rule
revenge	Milton
root of all evil	Bible
Safety in numbers	Bible
Second thoughts are best	Dryden
See Naples and die	Byron
'Sewing?' 'No, reaping'	Bottomley
Shakespeare, I come	Dreiser
Sheep in sheep's clothing	Churchill
Shopkeepers, a nation of	Napoleon
Shut your eyes	Anon.
The silver plate on a coffin	Disraeli
Skin of my teeth	Bible
slums	Agnew
Small but perfectly formed	Private Eye
Small Earthquake in Chile	Cockburn
Smoke-filled room	Harding
soldiers, effect on the enemy	Wellington

Some Mothers Do 'Ave 'Em	Crawford
Something must be done	Windsor
Spaniards, to thrash the	Drake
Spare the rod	Bible
Squeeze . . . till the pips squeak	Geddes
Star Trek	Kirk
State, The	Louis XIV, Napoleon
statistics	Twain
Sublime to the ridiculous	Napoleon
Sun never sets	North
Survival of the fittest	Darwin
surviving	Galileo
taxation	Otis, Reagan
Technological revolution	Wilson, H.
television	Scott, C. P.
Tell it to the Marines!	Pepys
Tennis, anyone	Bogart
timidity	Steffens
That's one small step	Armstrong, N.
There's is much that divides us	Reagan
They shall not pass	Pétain
Thou hast conquered	Julian
To my daughter Leonora	Wodehouse
To the manor born	Shakespeare
To the victor . . . the spoils	Jackson
toasts	Decatur, Golden Rule
Too clever by half	Salisbury
Too fucking busy	Parker
Tory Party at prayer	Disraeli
treason	Henry
Triumph of evil	Burke
Trust in God	Cromwell

truth/truths	Armstrong, Sir R.; Jefferson, Patmore, Reagan
Truth is stranger than fiction	Burke
Unacceptable face of capitalism	Heath
Up, Guards, and at 'em	Wellington
United Nations	Churchill
Unites States of America	Kissinger
valets	de Sévigné
vanity	MacArthur
Verbal contract	Goldwyn
Victorian	Anon. Dickens, Disraeli, North, Victoria
victory, paternity of	Kennedy
victory, tragedy of	Wellington
virgin birth	Jenkins
votes	Baldwin, Kennedy
Wages of gin is breath	Mizner
Wagner's music	Twain
Walk softly	Roosevelt, T.
wallpaper	Wilde
war	Clausewitz, Wellington
War and Peace	Bellow
War is Hell	Sherman
War to end wars	George, D. L.
Wassermann test	Parker
Waterloo, battle of	Washington
We are the masters now	Shawcross
We are not amused	Victoria
We never closed	Van Damm
weather, the	Rogers, Twain

wedding cake	Longworth
Westerns (films)	Agnew
What's good for General Motors	Wilson, C. E.
What's the matter, Mata?	Navarro
When I hear the word 'culture'	Goering
When the going gets tough	Rockne
White House, red flag over	Zinoviev
Why swop donkeys	Birkenhead
Wind of change	Macmillan
winning/victory	Durocher, Disraeli, Drake, Jackson, Kennedy
wisdom	Xenophanes
The wisest fool	Henri IV
wives	Bible, Byron
Woman is only a woman	Churchill
women	Addison, Congreve
Woodman, spare that tree	Morris
Work is the curse	Wilde
You can fool all of the people	Barnum
You can't be too rich	Windsor, Duchess of
You dirty rat!	Cagney
youth	Pitt the Elder, Spencer
You've never had it so good	Macmillan
Z-grams	Kissinger
Zulus	Bellow

SOURCE NOTES

1 A letter to Bishop Mandell Creighton of 2 April 1887. Louise Creighton, *The Life And Letters Of Mandell Creighton: By His Wife*, London, Longmans Green, 1904.

2 Louise Creighton, *The Life And Letters Of Mandell Creighton: By His Wife*, London, Longmans Green, 1904, vol. II, p. 503.

3 Gertrude Himmelfarb, *On Liberty and Liberalism: The Case of John Stuart Mill*, New York, Alfred A. Knopf, 1974.

4 Douglas Cater, *Dana: The Irrelevant Man*, New York, McGraw Hill, 1970.

5 Joseph Addison, *Cato* (1713), Act IV, scene i.

6 *Encyclopaedia Britannica*, 11th edn, vol. 1, pp. 276–7.

7 *See* Sir Paul Harvey *Oxford Companion*, p. 490 *and* Andrew Lang *History of English Literature*, London, Longmans, 1912, pp. 118–20.

8 Melinda Corey & George Ochoa, *American History: The New York Library Book of Answers*, New York, Stonehouse, 1993, p. 129.

9 Quoted by the *Detroit Free Press*, 19 October 1968.

10 Katherine Whitehorn, *Sunday Best*, London, Eyre Methuen, 1976, 'Decoding The West'.

11 George Sullivan, *The Cassius Clay Story*, New York, Fleet, 1964, ch. 5.

12 Colin Jarman, *I Said It My Way*, p. 22.

13 Quoted by J. Garthorne-Hardy, *The Rise and Fall of the British Nanny*, London, Hodder & Stoughton, 1972, ch. 3.

14 Colin Jarman, *I Said It My Way*, p. 28.

15 It still took eleven days between Armstrong setting foot on the moon on 20 July 1969 and the *New York Times* correcting his historic quotation on 31 July.

16 *Daily Mail*, Answers to Correspondents, Monday 12 September 1994.

17 Edmund Burke on the economy of truth.

18 Plato, *The Republic*, book II.

19 Mark Twain, *Following The Equator*, New York, P. F. Collins, 1897, ch. 7. Twain used this sentiment several times in slightly different forms.

20 Per Revd William Oddie, the *Sunday Times*, 13 March 1994.

21 A. S. E. Ackerman, *Popular Fallacies*, p. 400, C. E. Clark, *Mistakes We Make*, London, H. Marshall & Son, 1901, p. 15.

22 *Encyclopaedia Britannica*, vol. VII, pp. 393–4. A. S. E. Ackerman, *Popular Fallacies*, pp. 399–400.

23 Alfred Austin, *The Golden Age*.

24 *See* James Lewis May in the *Dublin Review*, July 1937, cited by *Oxford Quotations*, 1942, p. 12.

25 Stephen Pile, *Heroic Failures*, p. 116.

26 William Mcgonagall, *The Tay Bridge Disaster* from *Oxford Quotations*, 1985, p. 325.

27 Stephen Pile, *Heroic Failures*, p. 125.

28 *Counsels, Civill and Morall: The Essays of F. Bacon*, 3rd edn, 1625.

29 Raphael Holinshed (d. *c.* 1580), *Historie of England*, VII, xiii.

30 P. G. Wodehouse, *The Reverent Wooing of Archibald*, from *Mr Mulliner Speaking*, London, Herbert Jenkins, 1929.

31 J. M. Keynes, *The Economic Consequences of the Peace*, London, Macmillan, 1919, p. 133 and R. F. (Sir Roy) Harrod, *The Life of John Maynard Keynes*, London, Macmillan, 1951, p. 226.

32 Letter of 12 February 1919 quoted by A. W. Baldwin (3rd Earl Baldwin), *My Father: the True Story*, London, George Allen & Unwin, 1956, p. 82.

33 Sir William Fraser Bt., *Words On Wellington*, London, J. C. Nimmo, 1889, p. 12.

34 Quoted by Tom Driberg, *Beaverbrook*, London, Weidenfeld & Nicolson, 1956, pp. 213–14.

35 Middlemas & Barnes, *Baldwin*, London, Weidenfeld & Nicolson, 1969, p. 600.

36 Matthew Parris, *Scorn*, London, Hamish Hamilton, 1994, p. 97. Parris wrongly attributes this comment to the 10th Duke who was only Marquess of Hartington at that time.

37 Second Earl of Birkenhead, *Rudyard Kipling*, London, Star, 1980, p. 301.

38 Quoted by J. M. Keynes, *The Economic Consequences of the Peace*, London, Macmillan, 1919, pp. 129–30.

39 *Oxford Quotations*, 1985, p. 314.

40 *New York Times*, 17 April 1947. Jonathon Green, *Says Who!*, p. 72, *Oxford Modern Quotations*, p. 27.

41 Brewer, 1894, p. 225.

42 *Chambers Biograpahical*, pp. 109, 540. *Oxford Quotations*, 1985, p. 229. Brewer, 1894, p. 225.

43 Sir Paul Harvey *Oxford Companion*, p. 103.

44 Hilaire Belloc, *About John* from *Cautionary Verses*, London, Duckworth, 1985, p. 120.

45 Hilaire Belloc, *On A Great Election* in *Sonnets and Verse*, London, Duckworth, 1923.

46 Humbert Wolfe, *Over the Fire* from *The Uncelestial City*, London, Victor Gollancz, 1930.

47 *See* Keith Botsford, the *Independent*, 31 March 1994.

48 Tom Berenger, *Playboy*, 1982, quoted by Tony Crawley, *The Dictionary of Film Quotations*, London, Wordsworth, 1994, p. 240.

49 The Bible, the book of Genesis, 6:19 and 7:2–3.

50 *Encyclopaedia Judaica*, vol III, Jerusalem, Keter Publishing, 1978, p. 290. Book of Genesis, 8:4. A. S. E. Ackerman, *Popular Fallacies* pp. 527–8.

51 The Bible: the book of Proverbs, 16:18.

52 John Heywood, *Heywood's Proverbs and Epigrams*, 1546, now in the Huntingdon Library, Pasadena, California.

53 The Bible, book of Proverbs, 13:24 and 22:15.

54 Samuel Butler, *Hudibras*, part II, canto 1, line 840–44.

55 Prof. W. H. Bennett & Walter F. Adeney, *The Bible and Criticism*, T. C. & E. C. Jack, London, 1912, p. 11.

56 *The Money Song* from Harold Rome's *That's The Ticket*, 1947, USA.

57 The Bible: St Paul's First Epistle to Timothy, 6:10.

58 Samuel Butler, *Erewhon*, ch. 20.

59 C. E. Clark, *More Mistakes We Make*, London, Horace Marshall, 1901, p. 79.

60 The Bible: St Paul's First Epistle to Timothy, 3:ii.

61 The Bible, book of Proverbs, 11:14.

62 I am indebted to Mr David Damant for reminding me of this.

63 The Bible: The Book of Proverbs, 12:10.

64 Alexander Pope, *An Essay On Criticism*, 1711, line 625.

65 The Venerable Bede, *Ecclesiastical History*, c. 735 cited by Brewer, *Phrase and Fable*, 1894, p. 911.

66 *Oxford Quotations*, 1985, p. 519. Bartlett, 1937, p. 138 citing Henri Estienne, *Prémices*, 1594, and Brewer, 1894, p. 529.

67 The Bible, the book of Job, 19:20.

68 Francis W. Hirst, *In The Golden Days*, London, Frederick Muller, 1947, p. 106.

69 *Oxford Quotations*, 1985, p. 84.

70 *Oxford Quotations*, 1985, p. 89.

71 Ezra Goodman, *Bogey: The Good-Bad Guy*, New York, L. Stuart, 1965, ch. 4.

72 S. T. Felstead, *Horatio Bottomley*, London, John Murray, 1936, ch. 16.

73 Larry Swindell, *Charles Boyer: the Reluctant Lover*, London, Weidenfeld & Nicolson, 1983, *Oxford Modern Quotations*, p. 51. Tom Burnham, *More Misinformation*, p. 52.

74 *See* the *Observer*, 1 January 1956 *and* Bob Thomas's *Brando*, London, W. H. Allen, 1973, ch. 8.

75 Edmund Burke, *Speech On Conciliation With America*, 22 March 1775.

76 George Gordon, Lord Byron, *Don Juan* (1818–20), stanza 101.

77 Thomas Carlyle, *Heroes And Hero Worship*, ch. 5.

78 Thomas Babington Macaulay, on *Hallam's Constitutional History* in the *Edinburgh Review*, September 1928.

79 Brewer, 1894, p. 1262.

80 Robert Hendrickson, *Facts On File*, p. 233.

81 John Gay, *A Ballad On A Quadrille*, and William Shakespeare, *King John*, Act IV, scene ii.

82 Johnny Weissmuller in *Photoplay Magazine*, June 1932.

83 R. A. Butler, *The Art of the Possible*, London, Hamish Hamilton, 1971, p. 183.

84 Jonathon Green, *Says Who!*, p. 150.

85 R. A. Butler, *The Art of the Possible*, London, Hamish Hamilton, 1971, p. xi.

86 Sidney Whitman, *Personal Reminiscences of Prince Bismarck*, London, John Murray, 1902, p. 252.

87 Samuel Butler, *Hudibras*, part II, 1664, line 923 and part III, iii, lines 241–4. James Ray, *A Compleat History Of The Rebellion*, printed for the author, 1755.

88 Nicholas Udall, *Erasmus' Apophthegms*, quoted in *I Said It My Way*, p. 48.

89 *Oxford Quotations*, 1985, p. 129.

90 Robert Hendrickson, *The Literary Life*, pp. 264–5.

91 *See* the *Daily Mail*, 28 July 1994, p. 53.

92 Speaking at the American Film Institute banquet on 13 March 1974. *See* James Cagney, *Cagney By Cagney*, Garden City NY, Doubleday, 1976, ch. 14.

93 Jonathon Green, *Says Who?*, p. 105.

94 The *Sun*, 11 January 1979. *See also* David Butler, *The British General Election of 1979*, London, Macmillan, 1980, p. 121.

95 *Oxford Quotations*, 1985, p. 128.

96 Fournier, *L'Esprit dans L'Histoire*, cited by Bartlett, 1937, p. 1061 note 3. Benham, 1948, 744b, says de Rougemont wrote in his *Journal General* (which might be the title of his column) on 24 June 1815. Dow Richardson, 'They Didn't Say It', the *New York Times Magazine* of 7 January 1945 uses the style Michel-Nicholas Balisson, Baron de Rougemont.

97 *Oxford Modern Quotations*, p. 249.

98 These quotes are taken from Boller & George's *They Never Said It*.

99 Thomas Carlyle, *The Life of Frederick The Great*, vol. IV, ch. 3.

100 Brewer, 1894, pp. 1254, 224.

101 Mr Justice Caulfield's summing-up to the jury on 23 July 1987, reported in *The Times*, 24 July 1987.

102 Lord David Cecil in *The Cecils of Hatfield House* quoted by Wintle & Kenin, *The Dictionary of Biographical Quotation*, p. 152.

103 *The Times*, 31 May 1984.

104 Earl & Countess Spencer, *The Spencers on Spas*, London, Weidenfeld & Nicolson, 1983, ch. 14.

105 That is, Philip Dormer Stanhope, the 4th Earl of Chesterfield.

106 Ferris Greenslet, *Under The Bridge*, Boston, Houghton Mifflin, 1943, ch. 10.

107 Jonathon Green, *Says Who?*, p. 522.

108 *Oxford Quotations*, 1985, p. 91; *The Writings of John Bradford*, London, Parker Society edn, 1853.

109 See *Brewer's Twentieth Century*, p. 300 and *Oxford Quotations*, 1985, p. 150, for these and other earlier uses of this phrase. Indeed 'iron curtain' seems to have been so widely used it ought to have been a cliché by the time Churchill spoke at Fulton.

110 Robert Hendrickson, *Facts On File*, New York and London, 1987, p. 541.

111 Rudyard Kipling, *The Betrothed*.

112 This remark was made by General Kurt von Hammerstein around 1933. It has been attributed to von Clausewitz, von Ludendorff and von Hindenburg among others.

113 Colonel Murphy discovered this earliest source in the Ministry of Defence Library in London, citing R. D. Heinl's *Dictionary of Military And Naval Quotations* published by the US Navy Institute at Annapolis. The general was properly von Hammerstein-Equord, but the 'Equord' is commonly omitted.

114 Mao Zedong, 1938 lecture printed in *Selected Works*, 1965, vol. II, p. 153.

115 Claud Cockburn, *In Times Of Trouble*, London, Rupert Hart-Davis, p. 151.

116 John Macabe, *George M. Cohan*, New York, Da Capo, 1980, ch. 13, quoting Cohan talking to a reporter about the show *Broadway Jones* in 1912.

117 David Owen quoted in the *Observer* of 28 April 1985.

118 John Wolcot, *Lyric Odes To The Royal Academicians*, 1782–5.

119 *Oxford Quotations*, 1985, p. 160.

120 Jonathan Green, *The Book of Rock Quotes*, London, Omnibus Press, 1978, p. 19.

121 Paul Davies, *A. J. Cook*, Manchester, Manchester University Press, Lives of the Left Series, 1987.

122 Reported in *The Times* of 5 April 1926.

123 Kenin & Wintle, *Biographical Quotation*, p. 193, citing the Congressional Record.

124 Bartlett, 1937, p. 819.

125 C. Lathem, *Meet Calvin Coolidge: The Man Behind The Myth*, Vermont, Brattleboro, 1960, p. 151.

126 Calvin Coolidge, speech in Washington on 17 January 1925 to the Society of American Newspaper Editors.

127 Kenin & Wintle, *Biographical Quotation* p. 194, citing *Crowded Hours – Reminiscences of Alice Roosevelt Longworth* and Jonathon

Green, *Says Who!*, p. 499. Sometimes the dentist becomes a doctor.

128 Hesketh Pearson, *Common Misquotations*, p. 29.

129 Letter to the General Assembly of the Church of Scotland, 3 August 1650.

130 W. C. Sellar & R. J. Yeatman, *1066 And All That*, London, Methuen, 1930, ch. 35.

131 Harold Nicolson, *Curzon: The Last Phase*, London, Constable, 1934, p. 48.

132 *Oxford Quotations*, 1985, p. 171.

133 Benham, 1887, p. 469.

134 C. E. Clark, *Mistakes We Make*, London, C. A. Pearson, 1898, p. 89.

135 A. L. (Algar Labouchere) Thorold, *The Life Of Henry Labouchere*, Constable, London, 1913, ch. 15.

136 Lloyd C. Sanders (ed.), *Viscount Melbourne: Lord Melbourne's Papers With A Preface by The Earl Cowper KG*, London, Longmans Green, 1889, p. xii.

137 Bartlett, 1937, p. 332.

138 *Oxford Quotations*, 1985, quoting Hansard of 26 February 1835, quoting J. P. Curran who, according to the footnote, had died eighteen years previously! Also G. M. Trevelyan in *British History in the Nineteenth Century*.

139 Matthew Parris, *Scorn*, London, Hamish Hamilton, 1994, p. 95.

140 Nicholas Comfort, *Brewer's Politics*, London, Cassell, 1993, p. 124.

141 Wintle & Kenin, *Biographical Quotation*, p. 242.

142 See *Oxford Quotations*, 1942, p. 136 and Dru Close in the *Oldie*, 4 March 1994, p. 32.

143 Jonathon Green, *Famous Last Words*, London, Omnibus, 1979.

144 T. K. Whipple in *Spokesmen* quoted by Wintle & Kenin, *Biographical Quotation*, p. 250.

145 From *The Spanish Friar* cited by Hesketh Pearson, *Common Misquotations*, p. 30.

146 Comte J. d'Estournal, *Derniers Souvenirs*.

147 Gyles Brandreth, *Famous Last Words And Tombstone Humour*, New York, Sterling, 1989, p. 28.

148 Leo Durocher, *Nice Guys Finish Last*, New York, Simon & Schuster, 1975, part 1, p. 14. Boller & George, *They Never Said It* p. 23, citing Kenneth A. Calkins in the *Wall Street Journal* of 7 January 1988, p. 14 and the *Daily Oklahoman* of 6 June 1986, p. 35.

149 George E. Allen, *Presidents Who Have Known Me*, New York, Simon & Schuster, 1975.

150 *Sports Illustrated*, 26 December 1955.

151 The *Sunday Times*, 4 October 1981.

152 Ralph Waldo Emerson, *Self-Reliance* New York, B. Tower, 1991 (first published 1841).

153 *Oxford Quotations*, 1985, p. 208.

154 Tom Burnham, *More Misinformation*, p. 37.

155 Richard J. Anobile, *Godfrey Daniels*, New York, Darien House, 1976, p. 6.

156 Tom Burnham, *Dictionary of Misinformation*, p. 123 and J. M. & M. J. Cohen, *New Penguin Quotations*, p. 332.

157 *Halliwell's Filmgoer's Companion*, London, Paladin, 1988, p. 413.

158 Charles N. Wheeler in the *Chicago Tribune* of 25 May 1916.

159 Jonathon Green, *Says Who!*, p. 302.

160 Anatole France, *Le Lys Rouge* (The Red Lily), 1894, ch. 7 and R. E. (Sir Robert) Megarry, *Miscellany-At-Law*, London, Stevens & Sons, 1955, p. 254.

161 *Tom Paine's Jests*, 1974, cited by *Oxford Quotations*, 1985, p. 4.

162 *Collection des Documents Inédits sur l'Histoire de France*, vol. 1, 1847, p. 129.

163 Bartlett, 1937 p. 1024, citing Henry Martin's *History of France*, vol. III.

164 *Oxford Quotations*, 1985, p. 139.

165 Palmer, *Historical Quotations*, p. 78 and *Oxford Quotations*, 1985, p. 185. Disraeli made his remark on 16 July 1878.

166 Polybius, *History*, book IV ch. 31.

167 Quoted by Thomas Malone in *Stolen Words*, New York, Ticknor & Fields, 1989, p. 99n.

168 G. Hills, *The Siege Of Madrid*, London, Vantage, 1976, p. 85n.

169 Abbé Augustin Simon Irailh, *Querelles Littéraires*, 1761, vol. III, p. 49 and Giuseppe Baretti, *Italian Library*, 1757, p. 52.

170 *Halliwell's Filmgoer's Companion*, London, Paladin, 1989, p. 459.

171 *Oxford Quotations*, 1985, p. 221.

172 Milton Vorst, *Hostile Allies: FDR and Charles de Gaulle*, New York, Macmillan, 1965, pp. 146-7.

173 A. & V. Palmer, *Historical Quotations*, p. 74.

174 *National Review*, New York, 6 November 1962 in an article, *Gaullist Apocrypha*.

175 Quoted by the *Cambridge Daily News* of 10 October 1918 and *Oxford Quotations*, 1985.

176 Keith Grieves, *Sir Eric Geddes*, Manchester, Manchester University Press, 1989, p. 72.

177 Denis Healey speaking at the Labour Party Conference on 1 October 1973, reported in *The Times* the next day.

178 Denis Healey, *The Time of My Life*, London, Penguin, 1990, p. 369.

179 *The Times* 21 January 1936, *Oxford Quotations*, 1985, p. 224.

180 Kenneth Rose, *George V*, London, Macmillan, 1983, pp. 358-61, 402.

181 A. J. P. Taylor, *English History 1914-1945*, Harmondsworth, Penguin, 1983, p. 110.

182 Rt. Hon. David Lloyd George in Hansard 11 November 1918, col. 2463.

183 H. G. Wells, *The War That Will End War*, London, F&C Palmer, 1914.

184 Quoted by Jonathon Green, *Says Who!*, p. 781.

185 David Lloyd George, speech at Wolverhampton on 23 November 1918 reported in *The Times* of the 25th.

186 Lady Violet Bonham-Carter (H. H. Asquith's daughter), *The Impact Of Personality In Politics* (Romanes Lecture), 1963, p. 6. Bertrand Russell, *Autobiography*, cited by Wintle & Kenin, *Biographical Quotations*, p. 454.

187 *Oxford Quotations*, 1985, pp. 224, 229.

188 *Oxford Quotations*, 1985, p. 283.

189 *New York Times*, 17 September 1987, p. 22.

190 Confucius, *The Doctrine of the Mean*, XIII.

191 The Bible: St Matthew, 8:12 and St Luke, 6:31.

192 The Bible: St Matthew, 19:19 and Leviticus, 19:18.

193 Cited by H. L. Mencken, *Quotations*, pp. 471–2 who gives some four dozen other examples of the Golden Rule.

194 Arthur Marx, *Goldwyn: The Man Behind The Myth*, New York, Norton, 1976.

195 Alva Johnston, *The Great Goldwyn*, New York, Random House, 1937, ch. 1.

196 Alva Johnston, *The Great Goldwyn*, New York, Random House, 1937, ch. 1.

197 Scott A. Berg, *Goldwyn: A Biography*, London, Sphere, 1990, p. 396.

198 Arthur Marx, *Goldwyn: The Man Behind The Myth*, New York, Norton, 1976, pp. 298, 10.

199 Norman Zerold, *The Moguls*, New York, Coward-McCann, 1969, p. 127.

200 David Niven, *Bring On the Empty Horses*, London, Hamish Hamilton, 1975, ch. 6.

201 Norman Zerold, *The Moguls*, New York, Coward-McCann, 1969, pp. 127–8.

202 Arthur Marx, *Goldwyn: The Man Behind The Myth*, New York, Norton, 1976, pp. 210, 270.

203 Carol Easton, *The Search For Sam Goldwyn*, New York, Morrow, 1976, p. 150.

204 *Oxford Quotations*, 1985, p. 232.

205 Robert Hendrickson, *The Literary Life*, p. 401.

206 Arthur Marx, *Goldwyn: The Man Behind The Myth*, New York, Norton, 1976, Ch. 15.

207 Quoted in the *Observer*, 9 September 1956.

208 Robert Hendrickson, *The Literary Life*, p. 400.

209 *Oxford Quotations* quotes Greeley, p. 175, in the 1942 edition and Greeley, p. 235, and Soule, p. 513, in the 1985 edition.

210 Tom Burnham, *Misinformation*, p. 98. Dow Richardson, 'They Didn't Say It' in the *New York Times Magazine* of 7 January 1945.

211 Confirmed by Graham Greene & Carol Reed in *The Third Man*, London, Lorrimer, 1969, p. 114.

212 Edwin Diamond, *New York* magazine, 24 November 1975.

213 Dudley Sommer, *Haldane of Cloan*, London, Allen & Unwin, 1960, pp. 318–19.

214 From Gore Vidal's essay *The Agreed Upon Facts* in *Paths of Resistance*, Boston, Houghton Mifflin, 1989.

215 The *Independent*, 12 January 1994, p. 15. *Halliwell's Filmgoer's Companion*, 9th edn, pp. 521–2, 670–71. *Halliwell's Film Guide*, 4th edn, p. 57.

216 Conservative Central Office press release, 16 June 1970, reported in the next day's papers.

217 Rt. Hon. Edward Heath, MBE, MP, Hansard: House of Commons, col. 1243, 15 May 1973,

218 Joseph Heller, *Catch-22*, London, Jonathan Cape, 1962, ch. 9.

219 The *Sunday Times*'s excellent 'Books' section ran a series on publishers' use of dishonest extracts from unfavourable book reviews, in the autumn of 1993. These examples are taken from the issue of 19 September.

220 *Oxford Quotations*, 1942, p. 563 and A. S. E. Ackerman, *Popular Fallacies*, p. 399.

221 William Wirt, *Patrick Henry*, 1818, p. 123. Stephen T. Olsen in *American Rhetoric* (ed. Thomas W. Benson), Illinois, Southern Illinois University Press, 1989, pp. 19–27.

222 Quoted by Kenneth Cmiel, *Democratic Eloquence*, New York, William Morrow, 1990, p. 56.

223 Dow Richardson, 'They Didn't Say It', in the *New York Times Magazine* of 7 January 1945.

224 *Oxford Modern Quotations*, p. 11.

225 *New York Times*, 19 October 1929. Jonathon Green, *Says Who!*, p. 259. Tom Burnham, *Misinformation*, p. 227. *Oxford Modern Quotations*, p. 94.

226 Herbert Hoover, letter to Senator W. H. Borah, 28 February 1928, quoted in Claudius O. Johnson's *Borah Of Idaho*, Seattle, University of Washington Press, 1967 (first published 1936), ch. 21.

227 Hardouin de Péréfixe, *Histoire de Henry Le Grand*, 1681.

228 David Halberstam, *Best and Brightest*, New York, Random House, 1992, ch. 20.

229 Boller & George, *They Never Said It*, pp. 63–4.

230 Robert G. Ingersoll, *Gods*, part I, p. 2. Eva Ingersoll Wakefield, *The Letters of Robert G. Ingersoll*, New York, 1951.

231 Alexander Pope, *Essay On Man*, IV line 247. A. T. Bartholomew (ed.), *Further Extracts From The Notebooks of Samuel Butler*, London, Jonathan Cape, 1934, p. 26.

232 Clifton Fadiman (ed.), *The Faber Book of Anecdotes*, London, Faber & Faber, 1985, p. 300.

233 Ivor Debenham Spencer, *The Victor And The Spoils: A Life of William L. Marcy*, Providence RI, Brown University Press, 1959, pp. 59–61.

234 Bill Bryson, *Made in America*, London, Secker & Warburg, 1994, pp. 50–52.

235 Page Smith, *A People's History of the United States*, vol. 1, New York, McGraw Hill, 1984, p. 271.

236 Rt. Revd David Jenkins writing in the *Church Times* of 4 May 1984.

237 Richard Reeves, *A Ford, Not A Lincoln*, New York, Harcourt Brace, 1975, ch. 2.

238 Dr Samuel Johnson, letter to James MacPherson of 7 April 1775.

239 Dr Samuel Johnson, Letter of 7 April 1779, to James Boswell from his *Life of Johnson*, vol. III, p. 381. *See also Sir, Said Dr Johnson*, compiled by H. E. Biron, London, Duckworth, 1911.

240 Thomas Gold Appleton, quoted by Oliver Wendell Holmes in *The Autocrat of the Breakfast Table*, New York, Sagamore Press, 1957 (first published 1931), ch. 6.

241 Anna Farwell De Koven, *Life and Letters of John Paul Jones*, vol. 1, New York, Charles Scribner's Sons, 1913.

242 Barry Phelps, *P. G. Wodehouse: Man and Myth*, London, Constable, 1982, p. 254.

243 Hesketh Pearson, *Common Misquotations*, p. 38.

244 George Orwell (Eric Blair), *Nineteen Eighty-Four*, London, Secker & Warburg, 1949, part 1, ch. 3.

245 *Oxford Quotations*, 1985, p. 286, credits Theodoret with inventing these words in his *Hist. Eccles.*, iii, 25.

246 Count Galeazzo Ciano, *Diaries*, New York, Doubleday, 1946, vol. II, p. 196, entry for 9 September 1942.

247 J. F. Cutler, *Honey Fitz*, 1962, p. 306.

248 Arthur M. Schlesinger, *A Thousand Days*, London, André Deutsch, 1965, ch. 4.

249 Charles H. Hession, *John Maynard Keynes*, New York, Macmillan, 1984, p. 207.

250 J. A. Stewart, *The Young Woman's Companion*, Oxford, Bartlet & Newman, 1814.

251 *The Young Man's Companion or Youth's Instructor*, Oxford, Bartlett & Hinton, 1828.

252 *Daily Mail*, 21 September 1993, p. 32.

253 As Mrs Malaprop from Richard Brinsley Sheridan's *The Rivals* would say.

254 Mark Green & Gail MacColl, *There He Goes Again: Ronald Reagan's Reign Of Error*, New York, Pantheon, 1983, pp. 36–7.

255 Hesketh Pearson, *Common Misquotations*, p. 48.

256 Revd Samuel Wesley, *An Epistle To A Friend Concerning Poetry*, 1700, cited by *Oxford Quotations*, 1985.

257 Charles Lamb writing to William Wordsworth in June 1806, cited by *Penguin Quotations*, p. 229.

258 E. T. Raymond, *Mr Balfour*, London, Collins, 1920.

259 E. H. de Mirecourt, *Histoire Contemporaine*, no. 79, Ledru-Rollin, 1857.

260 W. S. Gilbert & Arthur Sullivan, *The Gondoliers*, 1899, Act I.

261 E. T. Raymond, *Mr Balfour*, London, Collins, 1920.

262 Arthur Bryant, *Stanley Baldwin*, London, Hamish Hamilton, 1937, p. 92.

263 William Safire, *As Lenin May Or May Not Have Said*, New York *Times News Service*, 29 April 1987. Morris Kominsky, *The Hoaxers*, Boston, Branden Press, 1970, pp. 27–35, 420. Boller & George, *They Never Said It*, pp. 64, 65, 72.

264 John Maynard Keynes, *The Economic Consequences of the Peace*, London, Macmillan, 1919, p. 266.

265 Sidney & Beatrice Webb, *Soviet Communism*, London, Longmans Green, 1935, p. 1036.

266 Boller & George, *They Never Said It*, pp. 77–94.

267 *New York Times*, 13 February 1954.

268 Michael Teague, *Mrs L: Conversations with Alice Roosevelt Longworth*, Garden City NY, Doubleday, 1981, p. xi.

269 Jonathon Green, *Says Who!*, p. 499.

270 The first attribution is from Dulaure's *Histoire de Paris*, 1834, vol. VI, p. 298, and the second from Dulaure's *Histoire de Paris*, 1863, p. 387, according to *Oxford Quotations*, 1985 and Bartlett, 1937 respectively. Boller & George cite two sources which were unable to trace contemporary evidence for the remark: Maurice Ashley in *Louis XIV And The Greatness Of France*, New York, 1948 and John C. Rule (ed.) in *Louis XIV And The Craft Of Kingship*, Columbus, 1969.

271 Benham, 745a.

272 Napoleon addressing the Senate in Paris in 1814, cited by Bartlett, 1937, p. 420.

273 Benham, 740b.

274 *The Biglow Papers*, cited by Hesketh Pearson, *Common Misquotations*, p. 4.

275 *Oxford Quotations*, 1985, p. 116.

276 Jonathon Green, *The Book of Rock Quotes*, London, Omnibus Press, 1978, p. 45.

277 Edward Bulwer Lytton, *The Lady of Lyons*, Act V, scene 2.

278 Frazier Hunt, *The Untold Story Of Douglas MacArthur*, London, Robert Hale, 1954, p. 266. Michael Schuller, *Douglas MacArthur: The Far East General*, New York and Oxford, Oxford University Press, 1980. General Douglas MacArthur, *Reminiscences*, London, William Heinemann, 1965.

279 Jonathon Green, *Says Who!*, p. 505. Merle Miller, *Plain Speaking: An Oral Biography of Harry Truman*, New York, Berkley, 1974. Wintle & Kenin, *Dictionary of Biography*, 1978, citing *Quentin Reynolds by Quentin Reynolds*.

280 Brophy & Partridge, *Songs Of The British Soldiers*, London, 1930.

281 Thomas Babington Macaulay.

282 Jonathan Swift, *The Country Life*, line 81.

283 Bishop Jeremy Taylor, *On The Real Presence*, V, part I.

284 Speech at Bedford, 20 July 1957, reported in *The Times* of 22 July 1957.

285 Harold Macmillan speaking to the press on 7 January 1958.

286 Daniel B. Baker (ed.), *Political Quotations*, Detroit, Gale Research, 1990, item 2379, p. 144.

287 Dow Richardson, 'They Didn't Say It' in the *New York Times Magazine* of 7 January 1945. *Life*, 2 November 1942. *Oxford Quotations*, 1985, p. 216.

288 Michael Heyward, *The Ern Malley Affair*, London, Faber & Faber, 1993. Robert Hendrickson, *The Literary Life*, pp. 370–71.

289 From an article *The Machines are Taking Over* in *Life*, 3 March

1961, pp. 109–17. This poem was actually written by a 'Robot', that is, an early computer.

290 *Oxford Quotations*, 1985 edition, pp. 328–9.

291 Groucho Marx and Richard J. Anobile, *The Marx Brothers Scrapbook*, New York, Perennial Library, 1989, p. 206–7.

292 *Oxford Quotations*, 1985, p. 333.

293 'I am a marxist' – of the Groucho tendency', a slogan which *Oxford Modern Quotations* (p. 9) tells us was used in Nanterre in 1968.

294 Pierre-Joseph Proudhon, *Qu'est-ce que la Propriéte?*, ch. 1.

295 Karl Marx, *The Eighteenth Brumaire Of Louis Napoleon*, 1852, ch. 1.

296 Quoted by Alan L. Otten in *The Wall Street Journal* of 26 February 1976.

297 *Joe Miller's Jest Book*.

298 John Milton, *Paradise Lost* (1667), book IX, line 171.

299 *Penguin International Thesaurus of Quotations*, pp. 548–9, entry 811.

300 George Pope Morris, *Woodman, Spare That Tree*, 1830.

301 Quoted by Robert Hendrickson, *The Literary Life*, pp. 226–7.

302 Bill Bryson, *Made In America*, London, Secker & Warburg, 1994, pp. 110–12.

303 See *Chambers Biographical Dictionary*, revised edn, 1972, Sir Paul Harvey *Oxford Companion*, revised edn, 1933, Brewer's *Phrase and Fable*, 1894, and A. S. E. Ackerman, *Popular Fallacies*, p. 398.

304 H. L. Mencken, *Chicago Tribune*, 19 September 1926.

305 Quoted by A. J. P. Taylor, *Beaverbrook*, London, Hamish Hamilton, 1972, p. 375.

306 L. Dalmazo-Auckland writing in the *Daily Mail*, 3 September 1993, p. 46.

307 Brewer, 1894, p. 397.

308 See N. M. Billimoria, *Proceedings of The Sind Historical Society*, II (1938) and N & Q, cxcix (1954), p. 219, cited by *Oxford Quotations*, 1985, p. 575.

309 B. E. O'Meara, *Napoleon At St Helena*, London, Richard Bentley & Sons, 1888, vol. II. *Oxford Quotations*, 1942, considers it more likely that Napoleon was 'quoting 'Sono merchanti'', a phrase of Paoli's; see Gourgaud *Journal Inédit de Ste Hélèna*, i, 69. It is thought improbable that the Emperor was quoting Adam Smith.

310 Bartlett, 1937, p. 240n.

311 Properly 'Roger de Rabutin, Comte de Bussy', 1827–94.

312 Benham, 738b.

313 Bartlett, 1937, p. 271n.

314 Edward Gibbon, *The Decline and Fall of the Roman Empire*, 1776, vol. II, p. 1343. Bartlett, 1937, p. 271.

315 Brewer, 1897, p. 962. Bartlett, 1937, p. 1048n. Benham, 753a. The footnote on 'Albion' is from Brewer, 1897, p. 27, quoting *De Mundo*, part iii.

316 Augustin, Marquis de Ximinez (1726–1817), *L'Ere des Français*, October 1793.

317 *Premier Sermon pour La Fête de la Circoncision de Notre Seigneur*, Metz, 1655.

318 Said to de Pradt, the Polish ambassador, after the retreat from Moscow in 1812 and repeated by him in his *Histoire de l'Ambassade Dans Le Grand-duché de Varsovie en 1812*, 1815, p. 215. Also Benham, 738b.

319 Tom Paine, *The Age of Reason*, part II, 1975, p. 20.

320 Harry Graham, *Ruthless Rhymes For Heartless Homes*, 1899, *Equanimity*.

321 Tom Burnham, *Misinformation*, p. 224–5 and Ogden Nash, *Collected Verse From 1929 On*, London, J. M. Dent, 1966.

322 Henry James, *The Madonna Of The Future And Other Stories*, London, Macmillan, 1879, vol. I, p. 59.

323 L. T. More, *Isaac Newton*, New York, Scribner, 1934, p. 664. R. K. Merton, *On Shoulders Of Giants*, New York, The Free Press, 1965. *Oxford Quotations*, 1985, pp. 41, 362.

324 Colin Jarman, *I Said It My Way*, p. 175.

325 Doug McClelland, *Hollywood Talks Turkey – The Screen's Greatest Flops*, Boston and London, Faber & Faber, 1989, p. 150.

326 Elbert Hubbard, *The Philistine*, December 1909, p. 32, cited by *Oxford Modern Quotations*, p. 147.

327 Letter to Arthur Davison Ficke, 24 October 1930.

328 Damon Runyon, *A Nice Price*.

329 *Encyclopaedia Britannica*, 11th edn: vol. III, p. 400; vol. XVI, p. 546. *The Harmsworth Encyclopaedia*, vol. 1, p. 144. A. S. E. Ackerman, *Popular Fallacies*, pp. 409–10.

330 Richard Hanser, *American Heritage*, vol. XXI, June 1970, pp. 54–9.

331 Bill Bryson, *Made In America*, London, Secker & Warburg, 1994, p. 38.

332 Christopher Hibbert, *Redcoats and Rebels: the War for America 1770–1781*, London, Grafton, 1990, p. 117.

333 Colin Jarman, *I Said It My Way*, p. 153.

334 Winston L. S. Churchill, *The Gathering Storm*, which was published both in the UK and USA. In the American edn, p. 85, Churchill quotes the motion in attenuated form. In the UK edn, p. 77, he quotes the motion correctly.

335 Details provided to the author by Kate Wilson of the Oxford Union Society.

336 Michael Foot, *Young Oxford And War*, London, Selwyn & Blount, 1934, p. 69.

337 John Keats, *You Might As Well Live: The Life And Times Of Dorothy Parker*, Harmondsworth, Penguin, 1979, p. 48.

338 John Keats, *You Might As Well Live: The Life And Times Of Dorothy Parker*, Harmondsworth, Penguin, 1979, p. 51.

339 Marion Meade, *Dorothy Parker: What Fresh Hell Is This?*, Harmondsworth, Penguin, 1989, pp. 246–7.

340 John Keats, *You Might As Well Live: The Life And Times Of Dorothy Parker*, Harmondsworth, Penguin, 1979, p. 49.

341 Robert Hendrickson, *The Literary Life*, pp. 181–2.

342 Alexander Woollcott, *While Rome Burns*, essay *Our Mrs Parker*, New York, Viking Press, 1934.

343 Marion Meade, *Dorothy Parker: What Fresh Hell Is This?*, Harmondsworth, Penguin, 1989, p. 231.

344 Major William Drury, *The Tadpole of An Archangel: The Petrified Eye & Other Naval Stories*, London, Chapman & Hall, 1904.

345 Ed Bartholomew, of the Royal Marines Museum, quoted in the *Daily Mail* of 30 March 1994.

346 *New York Tribune*, 6 September 1917. *Oxford Quotations*, 1985, p. 517. Dow Richardson, 'They Didn't Say It' in the *New York Times Magazine* of 7 January 1945.

347 Jonathon Green, *Says Who!*, p. 622. *Oxford Quotations*, 1985, p. 363.

348 Bartlett, 1897, p. 319.

349 S. Gordon, *Our Parliament*, London, Hansard Society, 1945, p. 119.

350 *Oxford Quotations*, 1985, p. 374. *The Hutchinson Encyclopaedia*, 1988, p. 934. Benham, 267a.

351 Edmund Burke, *Speech On American Taxation*, 1774.

352 Alexander Pope, *An Essay On Criticism* (1711), line 215.

353 Alexander Pope, *Epistle to Dr Arbuthnot*, line 193, (1735).

354 Alexander Pope, *Essay On Man*, 1732–4, Epistle II, i, i.

355 Aldous Huxley, *Crome Yellow*, London, Chatto & Windus, 1921, ch. 28.

356 Fotheringham, *History of the Siege of Boston*, 1873, ch. 5, per *Oxford Quotations*, 1985, p. 403. Also Tom Burnham, *Misinformation*, pp. 69–70.

357 Dale Kramer, *Ross and The New Yorker*, London: Victor Gollancz, 1952, ch. 13.

358 Alfred Duff Cooper to Lady Diana Manners, October 1914, quoted by Artemis Cooper in *A Durable Fire*, London, Collins, 1983, p. 17.

359 Ralph Nevill, *The World Of Fashion 1837–1922*, London, Methuen, 1923, p. 347.

360 A. S. E. Ackerman, *Popular Fallacies*, p. 808, quoting Prof. Ernest Weekley's *Etymological Dictionary Of Modern English*, London, John Murray, 1921.

361 Francis Quarles, *Emblems*, 1635.

362 David Olive, *Political Babble*, New York, John Wiley, 1992, pp. 143, 200.

363 Quoted by the *Observer*, 26 April 1981.

364 Benham, 1948, 740a.

365 Mark Green & Gail MacColl, *There He Goes Again: Ronald Reagan's Reign of Error*, New York, Pantheon Books, 1983, p. 95.

366 William Lutz, *Doublespeak*, New York, Harper & Row, 1989, p. 293.

367 Jack Dempsey, *The Name's Dempsey*, New York, Harper & Row, 1977.

368 The Bible: the book of Micah, 4:iii.

369 R. Nevill & C. E. Jerningham, *Piccadilly To Pall Mall*, London, Duckworth, 1908, p. 94.

370 J. H. Cutler, *Honey Fitz*, 1962, p. 291.

371 Jonathon Green, *Says Who!*, pp. 334–5. Robert Hendrickson, *Facts On File*, p. 568.

372 *The Saturday Evening Post*, 6 November 1926.

373 Richard Hanser, *Of Deathless Remarks* in *American Heritage*, vol. XXI, June 1970, p. 58, cited by Boller & George, *They Never Said It*, p. 113.

374 Dow Richardson, 'They Didn't Say It' in the *New York Times Magazine* of 7 January 1945.

375 Boller & George, *They Never Said It*, pp. 113–14.

376 Theodore Roosevelt, speaking at the Minnesota State Fair, 2 September 1901.

377 Jonathon Green, *Says Who!*, p. 705.

378 Alan Wood, *Bertrand Russell: Passionate Sceptic*, London, George Allen & Unwin, 1957, p. 103.

379 *Hansard* (House of Lords), 7 March 1961, col. 307.

380 *C. P. Scott: 1846–1932*, Frederick Muller, London, 1946.

381 Benham, 1948, 793a. Bartlett, 1937, p. 310 and p. 443. Re Commodore Josiah Tattnall *see Encyclopaedia Britannica*, vol. XXVI, p. 451. A. S. E. Ackerman, *Popular Fallacies*, pp. 410–11. Allan Ramsay, *A Collection Of Scots Proverbs*, 1st edn 1737, later edn 1797. John Ray, *A Compleat Collection of English Proverbs*, 1st edn 1670, later edns 1742, 1767, *et cetera*.

382 Mme Anne-Marie Corneul, *Lettres de Mille Aisse*, xii, 13 April, 1728

383 Lord Byron, *Beppo* (1818), stanza 19.

384 Arthur Dasent, *Piccadilly In Three Centuries*, London, Macmillan, 1920, pp. 231–2.

385 William Shakespeare, *Hamlet: Prince of Denmark*, Act IV, vii, line 201.

386 William Shakespeare, *Hamlet: Prince of Denmark*, Act II, scene ii, line 205.

387 William Shakespeare, *Hamlet: Prince of Denmark*, Act II, scene ii, line 465.

388 William Shakespeare, *The Merchant of Venice*, Act II, scene vii.

389 John Heywood (c. 1497–1580), *Heywood's Proverbs*, 1546.

390 Thomas Tyrwhitt (1730–86), the authority on Chaucer.

391 Bartlett, 1887, pp. 635–6.

392 William Shakespeare, *King John*, Act III, scene ii, line 9.

393 *Henry IV, part I*.

394 See most biographies of Goldwyn such as Alva Johnson's *The Great Goldwyn*, New York, Random House, 1937 or Norman Zerold's *The Moguls*, New York, Coward-McCann, 1969.

395 Adam Smith, *An Inquiry Into The Nature And Causes Of The Wealth Of Nations*, 1776.

396 Hesketh Pearson, *Bernard Shaw*, London, Collins, 1942, p. 310.

397 Burton Stevenson, *The Home Book of Quotations*, p. 976. Benham, 1948, 497a.

398 Thomas Moore, *Memoirs of The Life Of The Rt. Hon. Richard*

Brinsley Sheridan, London, Longmans, 1925, 3rd edn, vol. II, p. 471.

399 Hesketh Pearson, *Common Misquotations*, p. 50.

400 Alain Le Sage (1668–1747), *Gils Blas de Santilane*, ch. XI.

401 Harold Macmillan speaking to a London Conservative rally on 7 March 1961 reported in *The Times* the next day.

402 *Oxford Quotations*, 1985, p. 506.

403 W. T. Sherman, *Memoirs*, 4th edn with an additional ch. by his children. Sherman's son was present when the telegram was drafted.

404 David Duncan, *Life & Letters of Herbert Spencer*, London, Methuen, 1908, p. 298.

405 'Conquering Kings Their Titles Take'; 'Lighten Our Darkness, We beseech Thee O Lord'; 'The Lord is a loving shepherd'. 'You have wasted two terms, you have missed all my history lectures and you must leave by the first down train'; 'Pardon me Madam, this pew is occupied, allow me to show you to another seat'; 'When the boys come home from France we'll have the flags hung out'. 'Our dear old Queen'; 'horn-rimmed spectacles'; 'a troop of boy scouts' and a 'well-oiled bicycle'.

406 The Cambridge *Echo* of 4 May 1892 supports the first two Spoonerisms. *See also* William Hayter, *Spooner*, 1977. Interview with Dr Spooner in the *Evening Standard* of 22 July 1924. A. S. E. Ackerman, *Popular Fallacies*, pp. 794–5. Also *Oxford Quotations*, 1942, p. 409 and 1985, p. 517 and *Oxford Modern Quotations*, pp. 282–3 and *Oxford Companion*, p. 516.

407 Lincoln Steffens, *Autobiography*, New York, Harcourt Brace, 1968 (first published 1931) ch. 18 and also his *Letters*, 1938, vol. 1, p. 463 writing to Marie Howe on 3 April 1919.

408 Bertrand Russell (3rd Earl Russell), *Portraits From Memory*, VIII – Sidney and Beatrice Webb.

409 Edmund Wilson, *Axel's Castle*, Charles Scribner's Sons, 1931.

410 Gertrude Stein, *Sacred Emily*, 1913, p. 187.

411 James R. Mellow, *Charmed Circle*, Boston, Houghton Mifflin, 1991, ch. 10.

412 Quoted by Nancy McPhee in *The Book Of Insults Ancient And Modern*, revised edn, London, Paddington Press, 1979.

413 Cleveland Amory (ed.), *Vanity Fair: A Cavalcade Of The Twenties and Thirties*, New York, Viking, 1960.

414 Jonathon Green, *Says Who?*, p. 735.

415 *Authentic Memoirs Of The Public Life Of M. Fouche, Duke of Otranto*, H. Colburn, London, 1818. *Chambers Biographical Dictionary*, 1972, p. 484.

416 Benham, 1948, 746a.

417 A letter from Lord Tebbit to the author, 23 August 1993. This remark is correctly given in Jonathon Green's *Says Who?*, p. 740.

418 Monseigneur Ronald Knox, *Essays In Satire*, London, Secker & Warburg, 1928.

419 Jonathon Green, *Says Who!* p. 741.

420 Joseph L. Maniewicz, *McCalls*, March 1975.

421 *Halliwell's Filmgoer's Companion*, London, Paladin, 1989, p. 735.

422 *Robert Morley's Book of Bricks*, London, Weidenfeld & Nicolson, 1978, p. 25.

423 Harry S. Truman, *Mr Citizen*, New York, Geiss Associates/ Random House, 1960, ch. 15. Harry Vaughan quoted by *Time* magazine of 28 April 1952.

424 Colin Jarman, *I Said It My Way*, p. 92.

425 *Brewer's Twentieth Century Phrase and Fable*, p. 232.

426 *Look* magazine, 3 April 1956.

427 Quoted by *Liberty* magazine in May 1933. Alienist meant psychiatrist.

428 Dow Richardson, 'They Didn't Say It' in the *New York Times Magazine* of 7 January 1945.

429 Mark Twain, *Following the Equator*, New York, P. F. Collins, 1897, ch. 25 and his speech to the 19th Century Club in New York on 20 November 1920.

430 Robert Conquest, *The Great Terror: A Reassessment*, London, Hutchinson, 1968, p. 92.

431 Vivian van Damn, *Tonight And Every Night*, London, Stanley Paul, 1952, ch. 18.

432 Alan Hardy, *Queen Victoria Was Amused*, London, John Murray, 1976.

433 Arthur Beavan, *Popular Royalty*, London, Sampson Low, 1897. *The Notebooks Of A Spinster Lady 1887–1907*, London, Cassell, 1919.

434 Alan Hardy, *Queen Victoria Was Amused*, London, John Murray, 1976.

435 James Parker, *The Life Of Voltaire*, vol. 1, 1881, ch. 25.

436 Stephen G. Tallentyre (pen-name of E. Beatrice Hall), *The Friends of Voltaire*, London, Smith Elder, 1903, p. 190.

437 Voltaire in a letter of 10 November 1770. Burton Stevenson, *The Home Book of Quotations*, p. 788.

438 Archbishop John Tillotson, *Collected Works*, vol. 1, p. 696, Sermon 93. Bartlett, 1897, p. 232. Stevenson, pp. 787–8.

439 Burton Stevenson, *The Home Book of Quotations*, p. 787.

440 Ben Jonson, *Eastward Ho!*, 1604.

441 *Walpoliana*, vol. 1, p. 881, cited by *Penguin Quotations*, p. 408.

442 The *Guardian*, 1 July 1963, reporting on the trial of Stephen Ward on 29 June 1963.

443 *Oxford Quotations*, 1985, p. 565.

444 James Thomas Flexner, *George Washington: Anguish and Farewell*, Boston, Little Brown, 1969.

445 Jonathon Green, *Famous Last Words*, Chancellor Press, 1993 edn, p. 234.

446 Boller & George, *They Never Said It*, pp. 126, 129.

447 Barry Phelps, *Wooster of Yaxley and Wodehouse of Kimberley*, London, 1992, p. 12, note j.

448 John Steinbeck, *Grapes of Wrath*, New York, Viking, 1939, ch. 18.

449 Count de Montalembert, *De L'Avenir Politique de L'Angleterre*, Paris, 1856.

450 Sir Edward Creasy, *Memoirs of Eminent Etonians*, London, Richard Bentley, 1850.

451 Sir William Fraser Bt., *Words On Wellington*, London, J. C. Nimmo, 1889.

452 Elizabeth Longford, *Wellington: The Years Of The Sword*, New York, 1969, ch. 1.

453 Frances, Lady Shelley *The Diary of Frances, Lady Shelley 1787–1817*, London, John Murray, 1912, p. 102.

454 *Oxford Quotations*, 1985, p. 567.

455 *Recollections by Samuel Rogers*, (ed. Wm. Sharpe), London, Longmans, 1859, p. 215.

456 Thomas Creevey (1768–1838), *The Creevey Papers*, 1903, ch. 10, p. 236.

457 A. S. E. Ackerman, *Popular Fallacies*, p. 799.

458 All of which appear, correctly, in *Oxford Quotations*, 1985, p. 568 except for 'Up Guards. Make ready', for which *see* Hesketh Pearson, *Common Misquotations*, citing Sloane's *Napoleon* and Sir Herbert Maxwell's *Life Of Wellington* (1900), vol. II, p. 82.

459 *Harriette Wilson's Memoirs*, London, Folio Society, 1964, p. 15.

460 Godfrey Smith, *Beyond The Tingle Factor*, London, Weidenfeld & Nicolson, 1982, p. 45.

461 *Halliwell's Filmgoer's Companion*, 9th edn, London, Paladin, 1988, p. 1142.

462 *Oxford Modern Quotations*, pp. 308–9. *Oxford Quotations*, 1985, p. 568. Jonathon Green, *Says Who!*, pp. 576, 781–2.

463 Mae West, *Every Day's A Holiday*, 1937.

464 Freidrich Nietzsche, *The Joyous Science*, 1882.

465 Hesketh Pearson, *The Life Of Oscar Wilde*, London, Methuen, 1946.

466 R. H. (Robert Harborough) Sherard, *Life Of Oscar Wilde*, London, T. Werner Laurie, 1906, p. 421.

467 Bentley & Esar, *Humorous Quotations*, p. 209.

468 *Brewer's Twentieth Century*, p. 109.

469 Arthur Ponsonby MP, *Falsehood in Wartime*, London, George Allen & Unwin, 1928, pp. 84–7.

470 Charles E. Wilson, testimony before the Senate Armed Services Committee on 15 January 1953, quoted by the *New York Times* of 24 February 1953, p. 8.

471 Jonathon Green, *Says Who?*, p. 794.

472 Thomas A. Bailey, *Woodrow Wilson And The Lost Peace*, New York, Macmillan, 1945.

473 William Safire, the *New York Times Magazine*, 7 April 1991. The book of Malachi, 4:2.

474 Sir Julian Huxley, *Religion Without Revelation*, London, Ernest Benn, 1927, ch. 3.

475 Saki (H. H. Munro), *Reginald*, London, Methuen, 1904, *Reginald On Christmas Presents*, p. 16.

476 Charles Keen reporting in the *Western Mail* of the 19 November 1936.

477 Jonathon Green, *The Contemporary Dictionary of Quotations* (1982) and *Says Who!*, p. 771.

478 Jonathon Green, *Says Who!*, p. 771.

479 Quoted by Frank Muir in *The Frank Muir Book*, London, BCA/William Heinemann, 1978, p. 115.

480 George Wither, *The Shepherd Hunting* quoted by Bartlett, 1937, p. 133.

481 Barry Phelps, *P. G. Wodehouse: Man and Myth*, London, Constable, 1992, p. 76.

482 Gyles Brandreth, *The Pears Book Of Words*, London, Pelham Books, 1979.

483 Barry Phelps, *P. G. Wodehouse: Man and Myth*, London, Constable, 1982, p. 99.

484 Bentley & Esar, *Humorous Quotations*, p. 221.

485 Howard Teichmann, *Smart Alec*, New York, Morrow, 1976, ch. 9. Tom Burnham, *More Misinformation*, p. 128.

486 Diogenes Laertius, *Lives, Teachings and Sayings of Great Philosophers*, *c*. second/third century A.D.

487 *Chambers Biographical Dictionary*, p. 285.

488 *Encyclopedia Judaica*, vol. XIII, Keter, Jerusalem, 4th edn, 1978, p. 470.

489 *John Wesley*, Sermon 93, *On Dress*, cited by Benham, 415a.

490 The Koran, ch. 9, per Benham, 509b.

491 Robert Hendrickson, *Facts On File*, p. 71.

492 The *Daily Mail* and *The Times*, 25 October 1924. The Letter was finally proved a forgery by Messrs Chester, Fay & Young in 1967. See *The Zinoviev Letter*, London, William Heinemann, 1967.